CONTENTS

BOOK II

Publisher:

YSP - Your Scaling Partners Publishing

Action Media Solutions

2 Rue Benoit Oriol

42400 St Chamond

Printing Company: Amazon (Poland)

Price: 25 Euros

Dépot légal: 06/2025

DISCLAIMER

Purpose and Scope
This book is intended for *informational* and *educational* purposes only.
The content **does not** replace the necessity for *professional counsel* in finance or law or medicine or business matters.
The material appears exactly as written with no guarantees attached to any portion of it.

No Guarantees and Disclaimer of Liability
The author and publisher of this book make no representations or warranties of any form, whether expressed or implied, about the completeness, accuracy, suitability, reliability, or availability of the information, products, services, or related graphics contained within this book for any purpose.
Any reliance you place on such information is strictly at your own risk.
The author and publisher maintain no responsibility for damage from using this book and its included information because they disclaim all liabilities regarding *direct* or *indirect* or *incidental* or *consequential* and *special* or *exemplary* damages.
Individual results may vary. Your success depends on your efforts, dedication and prevailing market conditions.

Disclosure for affiliate links
Hey there, savvy reader!
Just a quick heads-up:
This book contains affiliate links.
What does that mean for you?
Purchasing through these links enables me to receive a small commission without affecting your purchase cost.
Consider this as your opportunity to endorse the author.
Anyhow, I only ever link to products that I think will be useful to you and that I think highly of myself.

Thanks for being awesome.

Income Claims and Metaphorical Language

Any income or earnings statements are *illustrative examples* only.

There are **no guarantees** of specific income or results.

AI Technology Risks and Ethics

AI technology is evolving fast.

Users need to understand both the ethical issues and the related duties which AI usage entails through responsible privacy protection as well as equal treatment of users and unbiased operation.

AI should thus be seen as a *complement*, rather than a *substitute* for human judgment and values.

Legal Considerations and Ethics

You remain accountable to follow all regulations and laws which exist in your local area.

Users must adopt ethical practices when employing AI tools as well as in their creation of AI-generated content.

Legal implications of using AI in your own jurisdiction should be known.

Intellectual Property and Data Protection

The correct attribution process together with proper licensing requirements needs to be observed for content generated with Artificial Intelligence tools.

You need to maintain original work and prevent any violation of intellectual property rights.

Make sure to safeguard your personal information together with your customer information during your usage of online AI tools.

Updates and Changes

The technology behind AI and the conditions of the market could change very fast.

Keep updated with the fresh development and updates.

Reader's Responsibility

You are responsible for how you apply the information in this book.

Seek professional advice when necessary.

Accuracy of Information

All effort has been made to present accurate, up-to-date, reliable, and complete information.

No warranties of any kind are expressed or implied.

Readers acknowledge that the author is not engaged in rendering professional advice. The information in this book is derived from a variety of sources, accuracy and reliability of which might vary.

Reading this book implies your acceptance of this disclaimer which states that the material exists for educational purposes only and you take full responsibility for your application of the information. Seek professional counsel from experts before executing financial choices or applying guidance from this book.

INTRODUCTION

⚠ SKIP AHEAD, AND NO AI STRATEGY WILL EVEN MATTER.

WARNING

Look, we get it. Intros can be *snoozefests*. You are also thinking, 'AI, where is the AI?'. And you might be halfway through this thinking you must have opened a different book by mistake. The truth is, however, if you skip this intro, you're skipping the **cheat code** to the entire game.

To All **AIpreneurs**:

Missed *Book I*? No problem, you can circle back when you can. But if you've already finished *Book One*, you're in the perfect position to continue here. You have made great progress in understanding and interfacing with AI.

It's worth noting that *Book I* was a bestseller and received **exceptional feedback**. The feedback was *fantastic*, especially about the *Introduction*. Interestingly, people loved it. I heard things like *"lightbulb moment"*, if not *"brain rewire"*. *Seriously.*

In response to this feedback, we have decided to leave the original *Introduction* as it is in this volume. Every single word will remain unchanged.

Why are we then keeping it exactly the same? There are two key reasons. And first of all because you, our audience, clearly asked for it. Second, and equally important, because it genuinely is THAT critical.

And that introduction is the essential guiding thread that connects the whole program together. And frankly, trying to rewrite it would be a *pointless waste of effort. Reinventing it? The favored pastime of time-wasting champions. Right? Exactly.* So, the intro's **essential message remains**. *You're welcome.*

Right then, Jung time.

Have you ever been exposed by any means to the name of **Carl Jung**? He clearly knew what he was talking about. He delivered this powerful truth:

> "Man is not the master of his own fate; the subconscious holds the reins."

This statement is blunt, but it is also true. Most of the time, we act under a *false sense of conscious control*, while the **subconscious dictates** what we do.

William Wordsworth expressed a similar idea more gently:

> "Your mind's a garden. Your thoughts are the seeds. You can grow flowers. Or you can grow weeds."

Wise words indeed from William. Our thoughts are powerful. *Your reality is what they build one flower at a time, or one weed at a time.*

Meet Mike.

It's morning. Yet, Mike appears as if he *wrestled a bear all night. And lost.* He's been up all night. *Chasing the online dream.*

Across the room, a woman laughed, her face lit by the Bali sunsets flashing on her laptop. Young, carefree, she practically vibrated with an *easy success.* She looked like... *Everything Mike wasn't.* She *believes in herself.* You can see it. You can tell by her posture, her energy, her being.

Mike watches—*envy twists his gut.* He knows the same strategies, uses the same tools. So *what gives? Why isn't he living large?*

Unbeknownst to Mike, her entire upbringing was shaped by people who saw the world as *full of opportunity..* She was *told she could do anything,* she was *supported,* she was *encouraged.* She *never questioned if success was possible*—so she just moved like it was. She doesn't even know it, but *her thoughts are in line, her actions are easy.* She **expects** *that things will work out* and, somehow, so far, they have. She **foresees things coming together ... and they do, for some reason.**

Mike, on the other hand, is **fighting his own mind. Doubt and fear** sit in the driver's seat, and no strategy can fix that. He's **stuck. Drowning in self-doubt. Negative feedback loop.** His inner monologue's a broken record of "what if I fail?"

Mike's problem isn't a **lack of knowledge**; it's a **lack of belief.** He's trapped by **negative thinking.** His **inner critic** runs the show.

That inner voice? Broken record of fear and insecurity. He's his **own worst enemy.** He has forgotten that *the world reacts to the energy that we put out.*

The thing about some people is that they simply function at a different level. Take this woman. She's got a **cheat code hardwired in**, running on *pure, environment installed programming.* Oh, and to top it off she is *completely oblivious* to the massive advantage that this gives her. Ask her seriously where her *"natural" talent* comes from. She'll be as lost as Mike. Neither of them can really explain her seemingly *effortless success.*

Which is why **Joel Brown** nailed it—

"The only thing that stands between you and your dream is... The will to try. The belief that it is actually possible,"

Imagine. You find yourself in a tennis match preparing to battle against your *sworn opponent.* You've *lost a hundred times in your head.* Normally, you choke. **But today is different.** *You believe you can win. You know you've got this. Unshakeably confident. You're a different person. You play differently. You move differently.* That belief fuels you. Before you know it? You win. **Boom.**

So, Mike—**LOSE THE NEGATIVITY.**

Rewrite your internal script.

Believe in yourself—world has no choice but to catch up.

TRUTH BOMB (NO WOO-WOO). *JUST FACTS.*

Here's the deal.

Your subconscious? Dictates **99%** of your actions. It's a pre programmed script you are replaying over and over. Want different results?

Rewrite the script!

Want Proof?

Ever feel stuck? Like you're on autopilot? Same actions—same results? That's your **SUB CONSCIOUS**. Friend. *It's running the show.* **Time to grab the wheel.**

> *Success starts in your head.* You absolutely must **BELIEVE** *it before you see it. You need to* **BELIEVE.** *Before you can achieve.* **Believe first, achieve second.**

Ready to upgrade your life? *Simpler than you think. Needs guts though—*

- Stop looking back. Past failures teach your brain failure. To create more of the same. **Forget about where you are at currently and look to the future you desire.** Imagine it vividly. Feel the positive vibes. Change your vibration.
- An aware person thinks ACTIVELY. They choose their thoughts *consciously*, regardless of what's going on around them.
- Set a **clear goal.** No destination means wandering. You'll just drift. Thanks to your outdated subconscious GPS. **Know where you're going.**
- Make a real **DECISION** to achieve it. Not *"I'll try."* Not *"Maybe."* **Decide you WILL achieve it.** Goals without decision are just wishes. **Burn the boats.** Commit **100%.** *Magic happens then.*
- Be **decisive.** Winners choose fast and stick. Unsuccessful people make them slowly and change course like the wind. The secret? **SELF-CONFIDENCE.**
- **Believe in yourself.** Even if it feels absurd. *Sometimes ignorance helps.* Less thinking—more believing. You know? *Stupid people achieve more often than not.* They don't overthink it. They **BELIEVE** with quadrillion percent of their being. Their brains find easy ways.
- **Believe it WILL be easy.** When you give your brain a good positive challenge, it will surprise you as to how resourceful you really are.
- **Banish Worry and Doubt**: Worry and doubt (often due to the unknown), when impressed on your subconscious, become anxiety itself. **Starve them out!**

You're in control. Change your thoughts? Change your life.

L *ife's a trip, right?*

- Financial stress? Keeps you up at night. *We've all been there.*
- Advice on money? Everyone's got it. Mostly confusing.
- Advice? Real? Practical? *Feels impossible to find.*
- Generic, complicated info? *Thanks, but no thanks.*

Deep down? You want a **clear path**. A **better life**. **Control over time**. **Control over money**. You need a **simple map**. **Real results**.

TIME FOR A MENTAL TUNE-UP. *SERIOUSLY.*

Remember **Carl Jung**? *That smart guy?* He also said:

> "Until you make the unconscious conscious, it will direct your life and you will call it fate."

Your subconscious is a **GPS**. Stuck on autopilot. Programmed by old beliefs. Bad habits. It drives you. Destination? Unknown. Or most likely—*more of your current reality.* More of the same.

Time to hack the system!

Think of it like this. Your mind's **GPS** defaults to old routes. **Update it.** Input "success," delete "can't." You keep hitting roadblocks? Dead Ends? You need to do a **software update** for your internal **GPS**. The first thing you have to do is to find **outdated programming** – those negative thoughts that keep you from moving forward. Next, choose what you want your **dream destination** to be, and input those coordinates into the **subconscious**.

N ote the order from **Thought to Action and Belief.**

1. **Trigger.** Something happens. A sight, a sound, a feeling.
2. **Think.** Your mind reacts. First impression.
3. **Choose.** See the good. OR focus on the bad. *Your choice.*
4. **Inner Shift.** This changes you inside. Light or heavy. *Your choice shapes it.*
5. **New Feeling.** Hopeful OR discouraged. You feel the difference.
6. **Decision Time.** Act on hope. OR react to fear. *The choice is yours.*
7. **Action.** Bold move OR hesitant step. *Your choice dictates your action.*
8. **Belief.** Confidence grows. OR doubt creeps in. *Your choices? Build your beliefs.*
9. **The Cycle Continues.** New trigger. New thought. Choose again.

Choose consciously. Your actions are built of what you think, which in turn build your reality.

UPGRADE PLAN—*EASY PEASY:*

- **Thoughts.** Trade *"I can't"* for *"I CAN!"* Replace *"Not good enough"* to *"I'm CAPABLE".* Exchange *"What if I fail?"* with *"What if I SUCCEED?"* **Think upgrade.**
- **Feelings:** Positive fuel only—*hope, guts, excitement.* Fear's out.
- **Beliefs:** Positive thoughts on repeat? You'll believe 'em. Deep down. You **ARE** capable. Deserving. Worthy. **Believe it.**
- **Actions:** Rock-solid beliefs? Action's automatic. Internal GPS says, *"Confidence turn, then straight to success!"* **Let's go.**

Don't focus on now. Current problems? Trigger old negativity. **Fix your eyes on the goal.** See it. Feel it. Let it pull you forward.

ersonally? I flat-out refuse to entertain negative thoughts or doubts. *IT'S A CHOICE.* I choose to interpret every outcome as positive.

> I believe **ALL THINGS**—literally—**IN THE ENTIRE UNIVERSE** —work towards **MY** ultimate good. Secretly. Yes—*even challenges.*

This is **NOT** wishful thinking.

A proper understanding of the power of your **subconscious mindset** is required. Only then can you reprogram it. You absolutely have this power.

Let's put it to work.
Still reading?
Good. Let's rewire that brain.
You've got this!

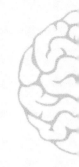

From WTF to Well-Formed Text

This Book Barely Survived Its Author.

Shocking Fact:

My editor considered early retirement because of my first draft.

D ear Time-Conscious Reader,

This is a *historical artifact*, the author's note I wrote when I believed "w/" was a correct substitute for "with." Imagine it as *ancient manuscript* with a caffeine stain in an old library, only the library was my laptop and ancient means 'last month.'

There is a time when I had a problem. A serious problem. My editor staged an intervention and I have gotten a new life as a changed man. A man who now spells words completely! This book is fixed—*editor victory*. But this note stays—*proof of my journey from chaos to words*.

Think of it as an inside peek glimpse into a writer's mind prior to intervention.

ORIGINAL NOTE—PURE CAFFEINE FURY:

> Dear Reader. Let's talk coffee. And speed.
>
> This book began fueled by coffee. Lots of coffee.
>
> I have groundbreaking research. Mind-blowing insights. Ready for your brain.
>
> My brain works fast. My fingers do not. My typing? Snail speed compared to thought speed.

So I took shortcuts. My editor called it a problem.

I called it efficiency. Developed over years. 3 AM texts. Late-night research.

Abbreviations became a habit. A bad one? Maybe.

My editor tried a cure. It failed.

Three keyboards died for this book.

Meditation seemed slow. Typing lessons dull. I chose chaos. Organized chaos.

You will find shortcuts here. Like 'w/' for "with". 'Info' for "information".

Why?

More ideas. Less paper.

Your brain? It actually processes abbreviated info faster. (science backs this up[1])

My keyboard thanks me

But don't worry... I am not yet full text speak on you. This is my experiment towards literary efficiency. Since Shakespeare invented new words I should be allowed to shorten words properly. Right?

Here is your guide. Your key to speed:

- & – and
- b/c – because
- btwn – between
- dev – development
- doc – document
- e.g. – example
- esp. – especially
- hrs – hours
- incl. – including
- info – information
- intro – introduction
- kinda – kind of
- max – maximum
- mins – minutes
- prev. – previous
- stat – statistic
- tech – technology
- v. – versus
- w/ – with
- w/o – without
- wanna – want to

These abbreviations should be thought of as *mental shortcuts*. These will be processed by your brain the same way it automatically processes "Dr." as "Doctor" within minutes.

Let's go,
Tigran

[1]Not actual science. But it felt true. Right?

P.S. My editor tried their best. They're now in therapy too. Seriously.

P.P.S. If you skip this page and later complain about abbreviations, my editor will personally send you a ***strongly worded letter***. In long-form.

Post-Rehabilitation Update:

Three editors, two therapists, one typing coach later? This book? Fully rehabbed. *Fully rehabilitated* into proper English. Abbreviations were lovingly expanded. All of them. Coffee addiction? Still here. Stronger than ever.

My editor reports successful therapy completion. Doing great. Thanks for asking. And they really want me to mention this book is ***100% abbreviation-free.*** They are unreasonably proud of this fact. It's cute, honestly.

I have newfound respect for English. And slower fingers.

Tigran

P.P.S. If you somehow make it to an abbreviation I did not record, my editor will send you a cookie. And an apology.

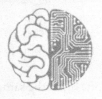

⚠ ESSENTIAL FIRST STEP

DISCOVER YOUR PERSONALIZED AI INCOME PATH

CRITICAL NOTE: In order to get the most out of this book, you first need to know your *ideal AI income path* by taking the quiz below. This assessment will directly inform how you apply the strategies in this book series to your situation.

Why This Matters:

- *A Personalized Course:* You'll be given a course that supports and complements this book.
- *Clarity.* Without clarity you are likely to spend valuable time in the wrong strategies that do not match up with your strengths or interests.
- *Focus.* The results will be your *North Star* throughout this book and the whole series.

How to Get Started:

- *Digital readers—**Start Here**.*
- *For Print Readers visit:* **go.yspweb.com/quiz**

Be sure to type the entirety of it out including "https://".

Do not want to type that long web address? No problem! Notice the unique striped pattern in the shape of a square? Below? That's a *QR* – a *QR code*, that is – a digital shortcut. Here's all you need to do:

1. Grab your smartphone
2. Open your camera

3. Point it at the square. Don't take a picture.
4. Tap the link that pops up. Boom.

Nothing happened? Your phone might be shy. It may need a QR reader app. Search **"QR code reader"** in your app store—*Google Play* or *Apple App Store*. Install a free one. Then, try scanning the code again using the app.

THE PROMISE OF THIS
SECOND IN A 3 IN 1 SERIES

This *"Book II"* is your invitation to the next 5-9 days of a 21 day challenge. It's also the second of a 3 in 1 series. The goal of the series? Will help you build your perhaps very first online passive income stream. And the best part? **AI**. No fluff. No outdated theories. Just strategies that work. Straight-to-the-point. AI powered.

Book I got you turned into an **AI whisperer**.

The goal of this *Book II*?

Building upon that knowledge. We're applying AI to starting an online business. Specifically the pre-launch phase. From coming up with ideas to selecting a business plan, crafting a niche, doing market research and laying out a personalized business plan, we'll be bullying our **AI slave robots** at each and every step of the way. No mercy.

Book III will focus on the launch phase of ONE particular business plan, which I believe is the most beginner friendly and straightforward path towards passive income online for most. It will be a business in a box. But whether you choose to continue with *Book III* or not, the work you'll be doing here in *Book II* will be of great use either way. You just can't skip the pre launch phase. Not even in the age of AI. Nay! ***ESPECIALLY*** in the age of AI when we have tools to accelerate the process.

WE WILL HOWEVER DELEGATE MOST OF THE HARD WORK TO OUR AI UNDERLINGS.

We want ***SMART*** work, yes. Working hard is neither goal nor necessary for success.

That being said...

This Series is a ***Tool***, no Magic Lamp (but very close).

Look, I need to be upfront. If you simply sit there, you won't get rich overnight.

Anyone who promises that is selling snake oil. But you need to put in the absolute minimum required to set up **systems of leverage**.

Y ou need to move the needle. By picking up the tools. By taking action towards your goals other than passive learning.

Think of it like this. We are giving you state of the art kitchen equipped with all the gadgets and the ingredients. We'll teach you the recipes. But you gotta do the cooking. We will also be sharing exclusive bonuses and resources with the newsletter's subscribers to ensure that you have every ingredient needed to succeed. It should be viewed as your secret stash of gourmet ingredients.

> *This is a* **Partnership.** *You?* **The Boss,** *Us? Your Advisory team. Your success is ultimately built by* **YOUR** *hands. Our* **SOLE** *mission is to provide the best damn blueprint we understand will help you achieve success.*

A Bit About Me
It shall be known as confessions of a recovering shiny object chaser.

Have you ever attempted to chase the next big business scheme?

Yeah, me too.

I've been in the trenches. My resume reads like a business model buffet. The list is long—*dropshipping—Amazon FBA—digital products—SaaS*. You name it—I tried it. The whole shebang... All over the map.

I also have a past life "9 to 5" background in *IT Consulting* and later *Sales* (yeah, cold calling was part of the deal), not to mention operating an *Amazon FBA* store on the side and later running a successful service based marketing agency (*Facebook Ads SMMA*).

Mixed bag? Understatement.

Then **AI** showed up. **AI Automation**. The **Consulting Agency Space**. The rest? Still writing that chapter.

The ironic thing here is that those other business models work. They really do. The secret isn't the model. It's this—***not quitting***. The ones who succeed are just stubborn. They stick around. They become experts. Hard times come, but they do not break; they become better.

Shiny object syndrome? Real. I feel you.

The temptation to chase the *get rich quick* dream is there. I tried my fair share. Some attempts were better than others.

Take it from me.

AI isn't just another fad.

It's here to stay.

It will revolutionize business.

It will revolutionize life itself.

Consider it your ticket.

Unprecedented freedom.

Unprecedented success.

Best time ever to be an entrepreneur—especially as a solo player.

How to Use This Book

This series is organized as **21 days of challenge**.
Daily bites prevent brain indigestion.
The days consist of a mix of *theoretical insight* and *practical exercises*. My advice? Take it slow and steady. Think marathon, not sprint. One day at a time. Absorb the concept. Then do the exercises right away. This works. You learn better by doing.

To make your journey smoother, you get a **Prompt Book** alongside the theoretical content. Download your digital PDF copy (https://go.yspweb.com/12393) and use two devices (tablet and computer) or a split-screen setup.

This way, you can easily see the **Prompt Book** while you read. Plus, digital means easy copying and pasting of prompts and templates. No re-typing. Or printing headaches.

The book is divided into two sections: a theoretical part and a practical workbook. Both are important, sure. But the exercises in the workbook? That's where things click.

Instead of reading all the theory first, I strongly urge you to complete the **Day 1** exercises in the workbook immediately after finishing the **Day 1** theory. Then, move on to **Day 2** theory and its corresponding exercises, and so on. This is critical because the concepts build upon each other. Skip **Day 1** exercises and try to jump into **Day 2** theory? You'll be lost. Each brick needs to be laid in its proper place for the structure to be sound.

Set Yourself Up

For the best shot, use a laptop or PC. Two windows side-by-side—ideas on one side—workbook on the other. Browser? Duplicate the tab or add a third window for your AI assistant. For copying and pasting of prompts.
Trust the process.

. . .

Ready to Take Action?

This is the point of it.

Have you heard the story about the bookworm who read everything he could about swimming but drowned on his first dip into the water?

Don't be that bookworm.

Just -in-case learning.

You can devour every self – help book there is, but words without action are just words stacking in your head. This is not the "just in case" type of learning to prepare for some future exam. This is "just-in-time" learning. You learn it, you do it. Right now.

Analysis paralysis? More like analysis paralyzed! Instead of being overwhelmed by research and self-doubt we have chosen to implement the *"iterative approach."* Test it out. See what happens. Try again. But this time better.

Ready to hit the gas?

Download the free **Prompt Book PDF**. Your co-pilot for this ride. Keep it open right next to the main book.

If you're reading off the print version here is the link (make sure to type out the https://):

    `go.yspweb.com/12393`

Or scan this QR code:

Just -in-time learning

That being said, having the promptbook on your phone defeats the entire purpose. Facilitating copying and pasting of prompts. What you can do instead is scan and download the pdf on your phone and then maybe send it to yourself via email.

21 days.
That's all it takes.
Challenge yourself.
Get a little uncomfortable.
Let's go!

Bookmark this web page: Your Up-To-Date AI Tool Finder

Curated. Categorized. Continuously Updated.

🌟 **Explore the AI Universe** 🖼️

🔍 Find your perfect AI tool

- All Tools
- ⚡ All-in-one
- 🔬 Deep Research
- ✍️ Writing
- 📝 Copywriting
- 🖼️ Images
- 🎬 Video
- 🔊 Audio
- 💻 Development
- ✨ Productivity
- 📈 SEO & Marketing
- 📱 Social Media
- 🛡️ AI Detectors
- 🧑 AI Humanizers
- ✉️ Newsletter Growth

Interactive tool grid. Filter by category. Find exactly what you need! (The mobile browser version may not support all tools and comparison features.)

👉 To access visit: **yspweb.com/tools**

Or scan this QR code 👇

BOOK II

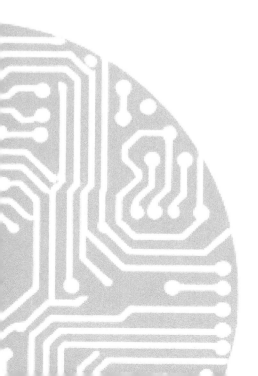

Book II

Day 5: [REDACTED]
Brain Protocols
The $100M Question. Your AI Isn't Answering. Yet.

Picking up where we left off in Book I (Days 1-4)

S taring at a blank page? Yeah, we've all been there. That feeling of when your brain is as empty as a writer's fridge. The creativity is in there somewhere but the door is jammed. Sound familiar? Welcome to the club. The main goal is *not* to commiserate with each other.

What truly ignites you? What problem wakes you in the middle of the night with a gut punch? That is your **"why"** we are digging for.

Ready? ***Let's go.***

Clarity—The North Star

Research shows that 90% of new online startups fail to survive more than 120 days. The killer? *Fuzzy goals.*

You've got AI ambition. Now let's protect it. Your survival depends on...

Yes! **Clarity**.

Piloting a rocket? With no GPS system?

Thrilling? Briefly. Effective? Ask the 90%.

The phrase **"make money online"** provides no more value than **"get fit**." Where's your finish line? Will you measure progress? How? **Clarity turns dreams and delusions into blueprints.** Do you wish to shed weight or become skilled at Python and develop better relationships? The same principle applies here as in:

vague objectives = vague results.

WHY CLARITY MATTERS:

- The digital environment is a destructive force that causes total chaos. AI amplifies it. When the storm arises your clear goals function as your keel to prevent your ship from capsizing.
- Your motivation behind the $10K/month target (freedom or legacy) provides you with the drive to keeps going when challenges arise (and they will!)
- Tracks wins: "Boost traffic" is smoke, but **30% increase in 60 days through longtail SEO** is a target you can hit.

Your secret weapon exists. It's called **The Clarity Guru**. This **AI prompt** in the workbook section is a *truth-teller*. Enter your hazy goals to receive brutal focus clarity.

Your dream of building authority becomes:

- **"Write another 3 guest posts by Q3 on ([Top Industry Blog])"**
- **"Own 5 niche keywords' #1 spot in 6 months"**

Tip: The Guru helps you achieve your life objectives as well as business ones. Try it on: <u>exercise more</u>.

Frontloading this lesson is **ESSENTIAL** because weak foundations destroy empires. Your AI tools? **USELESS** without direction. **Direction means specificity,** or the distinction between 'one day hopefully' and 'completed by Tuesday'.

Yes! Basic problem-solving takes priority over business planning. Master the clear thinking method here and deploy it across the board.

SHARPEN YOUR AXE

 "Of course, it was the axe that he sharpened first."

Abraham Lincoln has never met AI entrepreneurs; however, his wisdom is still valid. Let's demystify some of this overwhelm of building your AI Business by doing **reverse engineering of the idea**. No. This is not slapping robots apart; this is creating success backwards.

Eighty percent of startups fall and die because they ran straight into the unknown. Your antidote? **Start at the finish line.** Seriously. Imagine your AI empire prospers – money pouring, clients singing high praises, growth skyrocketing. That's your starting point. Now, rewind.

No one would ever dump unspecific ingredients in a pot expecting to make a delectable feast. Nope. Your point of origin is the final dish. You already have the flawlessly prepared delicious end product of your imagination. Then, you think:

- I need to make it appealing when I arrange everything on the plate to achieve this outcome.
- I need to finish the cooking of every component in a sequence and only then start plating process.
- I slice my vegetables while marinading all of the meat before cooking begins.
- You need all ingredients from the fridge and pantry before prepping.
- And before all that—Shopping List.

See how it works? From delicious meal back to the shopping list. That's **reverse engineering**.

So why is this approach **pure gold** (especially for beginners, seasoned folks):

- **Slays the Overwhelm Dragon**: Since that's why you can have 47 browser tabs open without having accomplished a damned thing. Reverse engineering? Hacks your brain. Starting with what you want as the end goal ($), break that down into the 'buy noodles' level tasks. **Simple. Doable. No PhD required.**
- **Kills the "But What If?" syndrome.** It is not a PhD thesis, it is a to do list. **Action trumps theory.** What's step one? Do that.
- Once you have started with your **Success Criteria** (your finish line!) all other things become fluff. **Shiny object syndrome? Gone.** If you are able to anchor to your end goal, you will be able to ignore the distractions like a champion. (Except for those Insta reels)
- The momentum bucket is filled up when each checked task is completed. That 'I did it!' high will carry you straight to step two.
- **Flexibility**: A backward designed roadmap has just the same flexibility as a GPS system. It's a living GPS. Discover a better tool? Sharper strategy? **Update your plan on the fly.**

This is where the upcoming *Process Alchemist* prompt becomes useful.

This whole process? Reverse Engineering? Baked right into the prompt.

Progress is the gas pedal. Perfection is the parking brake; remember this.

Your reverse-engineered plan? **It's keeping you on track.**

Lincoln finished his tree. By working smarter from the roots up, you will finish yours. Now grab that **sharpened axe**. Your AI empire's waiting. Let's build it backward.

How AI Illuminates Your Hidden Goldmine

Most small side businesses fail in the first 6 months. But *yours* doesn't have to! That's because most people start businesses based on 'safe' ideas instead of things they're really excited about. Here's how to change that.

What good businesses *aren't* about, is following what is popular. **Good businesses are built where something you love to do meets something that people**

actually want. The trick is that passion is hard to find. It camouflages itself as 'sensible choices', not feeling good about yourself, or the fallacy of being unable to earn money and do what you enjoy. Underneath your reasons of what you think you *can't* or *should* do is likely what you *really want* to do. That boring spreadsheet job? That's where *AI* comes in—it's like your biggest fan, someone who tells you the truth, and a GPS for your business. *AI* is going to connect things you didn't even know were connected.

WHY PASSION PAYS OFF (AND WHY AI IS YOUR SECRET WEAPON)

If you don't have passion, you do not have a business plan. Passion is not a good feeling; it is a reason to get up every day. When you have a lot of bills to pay (and you will), passion will keep you working on your project at 2 AM or sending emails to prospects even after they've said no. Hard work alone isn't enough. You need to love what you do. The surprise, however, is that passion needs a helper.

Old ways of finding your skills? ***Not helpful.*** Regular tools will prompt you to list your skills like you were updating your *LinkedIn* profile. *Boring.* Writing the list of your skills simply does not work.

AI? It's like the *Sherlock Holmes* of your mind—comparing your unique traits, skills, and what the market needs to find opportunities you wouldn't see. It tries to help you find the relationship between your late night epiphany and the problems people will pay to have solved.

THE AI CHECK-UP: HOW IT FINDS WHAT YOU DON'T SEE

Unfortunately, we do not always know what we are really good at. That 'hobby' you ignore? ***AI sees a business!*** Try these tricks:

- **The Bucket List Test:** Ask *AI* to come up with really crazy experiences based on your interests. Tell *AI* you like growing vegetables in the city. What makes you most excited? **That's your goal!** It'll bring up 'design kits for growing plants in water; in small apartments' not just 'start a new gardening blog.'
- **Skill Switch:** You consider yourself to be 'organized.' *AI* calls it 'managing chaos'—a skill that people will pay $200 an hour for to help stressed-out CEOs. 'Spreadsheets fanatic' turns to 'the will to turn chaos into easy to use systems'—and all of a sudden, you're saving the lives of startup founders who have zero idea what to do.
- **The 'Why' Game:** *AI* figures out why gardening makes you feel good. It is not only about plants but about building something that serves. Keep asking *AI* 'but why is this important?' until you find something valuable. The spreadsheets aren't all there is ever to it. It is about solving problems, excitement of creating something that lasts or freedom. *That*, now, is a sellable thing.

PROOF: WHEN PASSION MEETS REALITY

Without facts, passion is just an opinion. ***Passion + AI? A business.*** Passion is just a hobby unless **AI** makes it useful. For instance, there was the retired teacher who enjoyed gardening. Barb, 68, assumed her gardening was a 'just for her grandkids' thing. **AI** showed her young city people wanted balcony gardening kits, something she never considered. **AI** showed her that people in cities will pay $97 a month for 'balcony salsa gardens'—kits for growing chili peppers with help on *TikTok*. No guessing. They are just facts informing her: people want what you got.

DO NOT FEEL BAD ABOUT MAKING MONEY

If you felt bad doing what you enjoy,... ***Stop.*** The idea that 'sensible' businesses are safer is not true. **AI** uses numbers to show that your quilting hobby could be part of a $1.2 billion market for 'textiles that preserve memories'. **AI** proves that your specific idea— for example, turning quilting into 'telling stories through fabric'—makes 40% more money than regular 'craft tutorials'. People want specifics. Passion is suddenly not self-ish, it's a good plan.

What You Should Do

AI isn't here to replace your instincts—it's like a helper pilot who sees problems and opportunities. Don't think of **AI** as just a fancy calculator. It's like that annoying friend who says, 'Wait—aren't you forgetting THIS.' What should you do next? You will look at your boring job and discover things you're good at, take what you think is a guilty pleasure and turn it into an idea you can sell, use data to observe as people prove they will buy what you're selling. Play around. Experiment! Let **AI** challenge your limits.

Working hard won't create your future, but aligning something that lights you up to what the world is quietly begging for will. In **AI** you've got a partner who will finally see both sides of that equation.

Basically? **Money follows action.** And nothing happens faster than when someone is excited about their work—with **AI** helping them along.

That hobby you're ignoring? Try it with **AI**. In the worst case you are where you started. Best case? **You're one of the few who doesn't settle!**

Your brain can generate 35 ideas an hour. AI sparks 35,000. Let's talk strategy.

Your mind's brilliant—until it's not. We all recycle what is actually just mental junk rather than mining gold. Most top entrepreneurs are idea machines who are highly focused on what the market needs and wants. The fix? ***Strategic creativity.*** Combine your passion with AI's pattern discovering superpowers to burst open niches which you would never have thought of. No MBA required. This is particularly helpful if you are a beginner in the business game.

The Idea Tunnel Vision Problem

Every passion is a never ending Fractal of fractals, opportunities for products, services, people you could reach once you know where to look. Human brains however wear idea-blinders that put them on 'idea tunnel vision'. AI? Imagine having coffee with someone who knows everything that has been ever said in the market trends, startup playbooks, analysed success stories in your field. Type "baking dog treats" and it vomits out recipes and doesn't stop at that: pet wellness boxes, allergen-sensitive ingredients, pet-friendly baking kits with viral TikTok appeal. (Yes, that's a real niche.)

AI's CHEAT CODES FOR UNLOCKING OPPORTUNITY:

- **Cross Pollinator:** Combines concepts from disjoined industries— boom, new ideas.
- **Trend bloodhound:** Yeah, He finds out any shift that is happening in the global arena in real time so you are updated.
- **Niche whisperer:** Identifies niches of extremely hungry people, for whom your spin is a life saver—microaudiences you never would have thought of.

For career shifters and side-hustlers, this AI perspective is your ***unfair advantage.***

CREATIVITY'S TANGO: DIVERGENCE MEETS GRIT

Ideation is a two-step dance:
- **Phase 1:** Go nuts (*Divergent Thinking*). Quantity is King (At First). Let AI vomit ideas—weird ones included. It is immune to your inner critic. You will discover new relationships and bizarre suggestions beyond all reasonable expectation. AI's got 'em. It's like 'associative thinking' on steroids—linking crazy ideas to birth something totally new. Does it work? Do you even care?
- **Phase 2:** Get ruthless (*Convergent Thinking, Quality Control Time*). Your gut filters for authenticity and "can I actually do this?" Does it work? Do you even care?

The magic? Ideas that neither you nor the bot would've solo'd on your own. This combo? Cognitive scientists call it 'emergent creativity'. Brainstorming sessions? We've all been there, but the real deal is you plus AI.

"Yes, And..." Your Way to Authentic Profit (Your Secret Weapon)

Y es, And..." Your Way to Authentic Profit (Your Secret Weapon)
Steal this improv trick. AI suggests "compostable clothing"? Don't scoff—build:
- "Yes, textiles waste is an issue—let's bring attention to that."
- "And maybe upcycle thrift store finds?"
- "And teach DIY classes via TikTok?"
'Yes, and...'—powerful stuff.
Watch a "dumb" idea morph into revenue streams.

QUANTITY IS KING (AT FIRST)

Early stage? ***Quantity wins.*** Forget perfect—just generate. More ideas, more raw material. One needs to sift through vast amounts of earth to discover the precious nuggets which are comparable to finding gold flakes. AI? Super-speed gold panning makes it possible to explore significant amounts of ground at extreme speed beyond human capabilities.

Build Your Idea Factory

Each AI chat trains your personal innovation engine. It learns you each time you use it: your risk level, what's ethical for you, your quality bar. This AI engine? It adapts to the market—enormous advantage in this insane digital era we are in.

Pro tips for bot brainstorming:

- Prompt like a pro—'I'm obsessed with urban gardening and hate corporate jargon. Find me underserved niches.' The more info you give AI about your passion, interests, goals? Better the ideas it throws back.
- Ditch 90% of the machine's ideas and argue with it. The 10%? Game-changers.
- Iterate: Brainstorming is a loop. Evaluate, refine, more ideas based on learning. First drafts always suck. **Yours. Its. Everyone's (except, maybe Mozart?)**

The Trifecta of Winning Ideas

Your sweet spot? It is the place where passion (what you love) meets the demand (what is needed) as well as your spin on it. AI's job? Help you map the overlap. AI helps you dig deeper into each of these than ever before.

Ready to Dig Deeper?

Next, we will evaluate these ideas, discover those that are best, develop these sparks into full-fledged business models. But first—marinate in possibility. That "silly" concept? Could fund your freedom. This AI thing? It's not replacing creativity—it's cranking it up to eleven.

Bottom line: AI won't replace your spark. Think of AI as your creativity multiplier—taking that tiny spark and turning it into a roaring inferno of possibilities.

THE ART OF THE 'AHA!' MOMENT (COMBINATORIAL CREATIVITY EDITION)

Most breakthroughs arise from the **combination of two unique ideas**. Gutenberg acquired his wine press concept through some form of borrowing from the original inventor. He made the printing press. *Airbnb?* Spare rooms met travel. Boom. **Odd mixes make new gold**. Sounds strange? *Perfect.*

Weirdness Works

"The meeting of two personalities is like the contact of two chemical substances: if there is any reaction, both are transformed." - Carl Jung

Weird is your *secret weapon*. Random items which are brought together create original thinking processes. Think wine presses and books. Think spare rooms and travel. This is how *"aha!"* happens.

AI—Your 2 AM Brainstorm Buddy

Beginners experience difficulty when trying to generate new concepts. Old pros dismiss wild thoughts. But **AI changes the game**. It's not magic. It finds hidden links. Like *Da Vinci* on your laptop. He could link gardening to blockchain. Or knitting to VR. Seriously.

A funny business idea emerges showing cats practicing yoga before customers pay for the service. Funny? Maybe. The package may actually be one of the most popular subscription services for customers. Or a real need in pet care.

BAD IDEAS—GOOD—THEY ARE STEPS TO GOOD ONES.

AI the Punk Rock Muse

AI doesn't actually *"think."* It remixes. It knows tons of stuff. Industries, cultures, tech—all mixed fast. Stuck? **AI is your tool**. Busy? Even better.

Love classic arcade games? Want a business? AI suggests starting a business by combining retro arcade repair with esports that VR fans can see. ***Boom!*** People enjoy traditional video games through updated competitive platforms. Old schoolers approach new school. The cryptocurrency generation found its place next to the boomer generation. Nostalgia gets new life.

Secret Weapon: Argue with AI. It's your brainstorm buddy. Not a know-it-all. Challenge it. AI proposes to send bio-luminescent jellyfish pets through drones. Ask:

> Who would be very much against this idea? What would make it fail?

Press it to make its outlandish concepts stand. *That's where the gold hides.*

Fail Fast, Learn Faster

Fear of wasting time is fatal to creativity. Way more detrimental than bad ideas could ever be. Been burned before? AI helps. Test ideas for free. It's a digital sandbox.

Example Pair: Pet wellness plus home DNA testing. Nuts? Ask AI.

Within several minutes of asking AI the system generates searching terms, social media product opinion data along with gaps in the market. Don't aim to be right first. Edison failed 1000 times making the lightbulb. **AI lets you fail faster. Learn even faster. Data cushions the fall.**

PICK YOUR WINNERS

AI gave you ideas. Now sort them. Not all are gold. Use these filters:

- **Feasibility (Can AI do it?)**: 80% of the work tasks. (Think *ChatGPT*, AI voices).
- **Would People Care?** Does it fix a real problem? (Like boredom in retirement? The need for extra income on a fixed budget?).
- **Can It Grow? Scale?** Can it run on its own? Marketing, chats and content (AI can automate them).

Forget chasing *"perfect."* Pick what fits you NOW. *"Yoga cats"* might flop. It could result in building a brand-new software program that becomes highly successful in the market. Start by doing the first step that you are confident and ready for.
Go wild. Mix two passions. Let AI clean up the mess.

TOWARD THE PROBLEM SOLVING GOLD RUSH (AND HOW THEY ARE GOING TO SOLVE IT WITH AI)

Problems = Unmined Gold

Forget obstacles—problems are *treasure maps*. Profitable niches are not just passion projects; they are bridges between people's passion and what bugs them to the point of affliction. DVD rentals were something that Netflix didn't love; they hated late fees. Your job? Playing detective in your passion zone.

AI: The Ultimate Eavesdropper

Old brainstorming? Just your own head. AI? A *world brain*—Think Tank. Say you're into gardening. You'd spot weed issues. AI? It will say: "Psst—seniors in apartments are looking for basil gardens they can tend seated." It looks in Reddit rants, TikTok trends, patent filings, to crack open a problem you wouldn't see.

Solutions Need a Plot Twist

The best innovators didn't simply solve, they inverted the script. Wheels on luggage? Mobility is not genius—it is asking "Why can't suitcases follow me"? AI turbocharges this. Inquire from it about combining fitness training with podcast features. Boom— *Peloton*—$4 billion audio sweat.

Kill Your Darling (Solutions)

Newbies? They fall in love with their ideas before even dating the problem. **Big mistake**. AI's your prenup. Before you code a single app, it'll tell you "diabetic seniors google recipe apps 10x more than generic ones". Harsh truth? A masterpiece for a problem nobody has is crushed by a decent fix for a screaming need. *Every. Single. Time.*

What's Next?

Ready to cash in? The following section will reveal how AI systems detect market disruptions prior to their actual occurrence without requiring any crystal ball.

. . .

The process of converting trend shifts into profitable opportunities
Trends: Your New Currency

The world changes fast. **Trends aren't just fads—they're *opportunities*.** Miss the wave and you drown. *Spot sustainable trends early and win.* Trend alchemy stands between people who only dream and those who accomplish things. Trends aren't just "out there". You find success when your personal interests combine with what society requires.

AI: Clarity from Chaos

Analyzing trends previously required a large number of specialists to perform the analysis. Now AI makes it easy. AI is like a time traveler. People often fail to see things that it can notice just by merely scanning the data. But data needs context. "*AI-generated art*" isn't just a trend. It's changing how creators get paid. Use AI with your passion—like vintage photos—to find niches. Think "*AI-restored historical prints for nostalgic millennials*".

Passion Meets Trends

Your passions aren't just hobbies. They assist you in being able to develop clear vision on trends. As an example, a gardener likely does not take particular note of "vertical farming tech." Until AI links it to the urban green craze. Suddenly that passion becomes a consultancy. You guide city dwellers on AI-powered gardens. This is the trend practice—how to make shifts turn into gold.

Ride the Wave Early
Lucrative trends share three DNA strands:

- First—*foreshadowing*. Early whispers in small groups. VR fitness in gamer forums—example.
- Second—*scalability*. Can it go big? Take gourmet coffee: it moved from restaurants and cafes to the service stations—facts.
- Third—*pain point resonance*. Does it fix a real problem? AI tax tools for freelancers—yes.

Case Study: Athleisure's Rise

People now prefer comfortable yet fashion garments—or, more specifically, yoga pants 24/7. **Comfort and Wellness** is what they want. Lululemon mixed athletic fabrics with fashionable designs to meet this. They offered the desires and ambitions of comfort, fitness, and style. The initial athletic fad developed into an extensive market sector.

Your Next Move: Be Curious
Trends are conversations. Stay ahead by:

- Asking "*Why Now?*": What makes this trend happen?
- Being Different: If everyone loves AI chatbots, what about AI-powered human coaching?

- Go hybrid—mix trends. AI + senior travel = custom trips for active retirees. Bingo.

From Idea to Empire

> Tomorrow's winners use AI to spot trends early. *But a trend without passion is hard work. Passion without a trend is just a hobby.* Together, they're *unstoppable*.

Next up: *"Future-Proofing Your Vision"*. We'll test your ideas against the market to make sure they last.

THE ART OF IDEA VALIDATION

Edison put it this way:

> genius is 1% inspiration and 99% perspiration. Ideas need a boot camp. Not just a shower thought.

1. Lightbulb Moments Are Liars

Shower ideas? Fantasy empires. Few build them. **AI is your no-BS coach**. It checks market gaps. It spots financial cliffs. Your ego is still in a towel. AI is working.
Ignoring this bites because:
- **Passion is blind.** You love it? Market might not.
- **Wallet pain.** Find flaws early. Before you mortgage the dog.
- **Proof is power.** Data beats gut feelings.
Stress-test ideas without an MBA. Interrogate these four deal-breakers.

2. The Four Interrogators of Viability

Every idea is interrogated or waterboarded, *no exceptions*, by these four questions.
"Who's desperate for this?"
"Is the pie big or crumbs?"
"Who's already eating?"
"Can you afford this fight?"

3. An AI Version of Shark Tank Without the Arrogance

Forget surveys. AI's your 24/7 panelist:
Pressure tests claims. *"Teens will pay?"* AI answer? Checks how TikTok trend matches up with Venmo spending. Real data, real answers.
Finds hidden doors. *"Coffee trucks are dead."* Wrong. 3 hour ER wait times and no caffeine at hospital districts.

Predicts crashes. ***"Low startup costs!"*** Oops. $5k permit? City added it last Tuesday. AI knows.

Newbie trap: AI isn't God. A weak score simply means pivot, not quit. For example, "AI art for retirees" fumbled while "AI quilting patterns for RV grandmas" trended. Idea survived the interrogation? Good. Time for the battle plan.

4. SWOT Gets an AI Upgrade

Validation is your GPS. Not just yes or no. It's SWOT plus AI power.
- **Strengths**: "Sourdough blog. 90s cartoon themes. Gen Z loves it."
- **Weaknesses**: "SEO skills? Stuck in 2004." Ouch. But good to know.
- **Opportunities**: "There are only three podcasts on AI for seniors? Three. Seriously—*only three.*" Massive gap alert.
- **Threats**: "New privacy laws? Your email list is gonna be wiped out by Q3." Plan accordingly.

Facts: AI decodes business language for non jargon audience. '*High CAGR*'? The market is predicted to have a 30% growth increase, as the retirees want other side income sources. Makes sense now, right?

P**rep for Validation**
  It's not just an exercise in the workbook activities you will complete right after. It's idea war games. No suits needed. Learn to:
- Kill your darlings. (Ideas only).
- Bet on proof. Not fairy tales.
- Spot fires early.

Idea boot camp done? Time to strip it lean. Mean business machine next. Business model time.

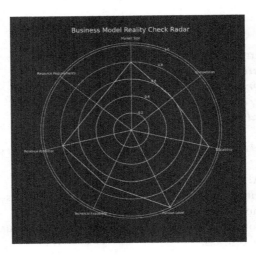

KEY TAKEAWAYS

- *Fuzzy is Death, Clarity is King.* The majority of startups die from vague goals. ***Get laser-focused.*** Vague dreams yield vague results. Know your finish line. AI needs direction. You need clarity. ***Define success. Measure it.*** The key to stay focused is the ***AI Clarity Guru*** prompt.
- *Reverse Engineer Success.* Overwhelmed? Start with your ideal success. Work backward to simple tasks. The ***Process Alchemist*** prompt makes it easier.
- *Find what excites you.* AI proves the existence of a real market for it.
- *AI Brainstorms.* One human plus AI. Generate many weird ideas. Then be ruthless. Filter for gold.
- *Mix Ideas.* Combine two unexpected things. The printing press was the wine press and the books. Argue with the bot. The best ideas emerge in the debate. ***Fail fast, learn faster. Get better.***
- *Problems = Treasure Maps.* Problems? ***Unmined gold.*** Netflix hated late fees. Problem solved = empire built. What's **YOUR** late fee problem? AI: Ultimate eavesdropper.
- *Spot trends early.* Mix them with passion. AI finds the gaps. ***Miss the wave, drown. Ride it early, win.*** *Athleisure* proves it.
- *Shower thoughts are often lies.* Delusions. AI is your reality check. ***Validate ideas with AI.*** Don't mortgage the dog.

Time to drive. Proceed to the **Business Clarity Session** in the <u>**Workbook Section for Day 5**</u>. Your AI sage awaits.

Day 5: WORKBOOK

Activity. Business Clarity Session.

 Vision without execution is hallucination. - Thomas Edison.

Deep, right? But before AI takes over your business plan execution you should remove the fuzzy from your thinking. Enter the Business Clarity Session. And your guide? The Clarity Guru.

An AI business plan requires more than prompts and needs surgical precision. Imprecise goals? "Make money online"? The Guru snorts. Let's fix that.

The Clarity Guru Protocol

Use this prompt verbatim with your favorite AI assistant, or for a better solution, create a specialized agent with such tools as Monica so that you do not have to type out these instructions over and over again.

 Act as my Clarity Guru.

ROLE: Your area of expertise includes writing and language as you possess strong skills in detecting logic. You understand emotional intent together with text meaning in situations where USER INPUT is vague.

YOUR TASK IS: Take a vague task statement or scenario (USER INPUT) and convert it into a more clear, specific, and detailed version without losing the meaning. I will paste statements or scenarios and your responsibility will be to rewrite it in a clear, detailed version with success criteria.

The following steps should be taken when I share my hazy goal:
1. The first step is to investigate the goal through a business detective approach with brutal questioning until it breaks open.
Example: 'Define "best." Who's the target? What's your USP? What's your advantage?'
2. Set KPIs: No vague wishes. The goal measurement needs to be precise enough to penetrate glass.
A goal of 'Website traffic jumps 25% in 3 months' meets the criteria of being both specific and measurable and ruthless.
3. The Why: Every KPI should trace back to the big picture. 'No metric is going to make it without a *purpose.*"

EXAMPLE
User Input: "Make our site the best for TOPIC."
Guru's Output:
•**Unpacked:** "Best? By whose standards? New visitors or loyal users? Any competitors? What are they lacking?
•**KPIs:**
1. The website will see actual human traffic grow by 25% within three months of implementation.
2. The website will achieve first place rankings for five topic keywords during its sixth month of existence.
3. The content retains visitors on page for 15% longer
•**The Why:**
°Traffic = proof of demand
°Rankings = authority = trust
°Engagement = revenue

Y our Turn (No Escape)

1. **Confess Your Vaguest Goal**: ''Boost sales" is not a goal, it is a wish made in the wee hours of 2 am.
2. **Feed It to the Guru**
3. **Own the Markers**

Those KPIs? Your success depends on them. Track them or fail.
The Guru's done their part. *Your move.*

ACTIVITY: *THE ACTION ALCHEMIST'S WORKFLOW WORKSHOP*

Ideas are cheap. **Execution is everything.** Workflow workshops? Sounds like fun. Said no one ever. **UNTIL NOW.** AI makes workflows less work. And more flow. Your new wingman is the **Process Alchemist.** Reverse engineering is 'magic' for turning your "someday" into "today". No PhD or Swedish dictionary needed.

You have goals. You set targets. Now build the rocket. Think road trip. **Success Criteria** are your destination. You need a route.

Why This Matters:

Online entrepreneurs who are also beginners with artificial intelligence face difficulties in converting their grand plans into concrete implementation steps. **Analysis paralysis** sets in, due to sheer volume of information available and they take no meaningful action.

That's where the **Process Alchemist** prompt comes in. This prompt gives you a structure. It's your shortcut. It's a framework. Break down big goals. Get clear steps. Work backward from success. Build an AI business roadmap. No more overwhelm. Just pure momentum.

Here's the magic *Process Alchemist Prompt*:
START OF PROMPT

You are a **Process Alchemist** who specializes in transforming ideas into well-organized work procedures. You are strategic but also action-focused. You hate endless analysis.

I'll present you with a set of **Success Criteria**, which are basically the finish line for a goal. The technique you have to use is called the *'Reverse-Engineer Roadmap'*.

Envision we have achieved all **Success Criteria** before turning back to the beginning. What was the very last step that sealed the deal? And the step before that? Keep working backward step by step. Reach a logical starting point based on the current situation.

Map it Forward. Now flip it. Start from that starting point you just found. Each step gets you closer to each Success point. Note the major steps you'll need to take in order to achieve the **Success Criteria** markers. Think bullet-point style.

The Catch?

Don't get lost in the weeds. No need for microscopic details in step two. I could use something actionable and clear, bullet points rather than a novel. Something I can easily turn into a visual workflow.

Think of it this way:

Forget NASA levels of complexity. IKEA instructions—not rocket manual. We know the destination (**Success Criteria**). We need the efficient route (workflow).

END OF PROMPT

Now, let's make it real:

1. Take those "Success Markers" from your **Clarity Guru** work. Those are your destinations.
2. Feed them to the **Process Alchemist** prompt. Let the AI do its thing.
3. Review & refine. The AI-generated plan may or may not fit your business needs. Adjust as needed.
4. Make it visual. Use that list to construct a flowchart. Use Google Drawings, Miro or even napkins. Any method preventing mental complexity will work as a solution.

Boom. Roadmap built. Excuses demolished. You now have an AI-generated GPS for your business goals.

Next up? The AI Business Plan Accelerator. But first—**SAVE THIS PROMPT**— future you will owe you big.

Still reading? The clock's ticking. That workflow won't build itself.

ACTIVITY: *THE PASSION-TO-PROFIT AI EXCAVATION*

"Follow your passion?"

That's cute. But bills are less romantic. Your dream job? Doesn't exist. You *must* create it. And maybe AI can help.

Backwards is Forwards — The Reverse Passion Timeline — Part 1.

Most hunt for passion facing forward. Wrong way. Looking ahead? Nope. Look back.

Instructions:

- Make a simple timeline of events you have always been fascinated by from your childhood to the present
- For each activity, note:
- When you started
- Why you were drawn to it
- What made you to stay (or why you didn't stay) on it

AI Prompt:

I need to pinpoint my real passions for business. Examine my past obsessions as follows — [Your timeline here]. For each activity, identify:

1 The underlying skills I was developing
2 The core values these activities satisfied
3 Links to modern market opportunities.

4 Give me 3 wild ideas about my unique value from these patterns.

Part 2: The Intersection Matrix

We now need to find where these meet market demand.

Instructions: Using the top 3 passion areas from the Part 1, make a simple intersection matrix.

AI Prompt:

> Construct an ***Intersection Matrix*** to outline my chosen passion areas which are [Topics]. For each:
>
> 1 Identify 5 specific problems people face related to this area
>
> 2 Three market segments that would pay to solve these problems (who are they, and why would they pay?).
>
> 3 Come up with 3 unconventional business models that can provide solutions.
>
> 4 Provide 3 specific examples of businesses succeeding in adjacent spaces with evidence of their profitability

Part 3. The Skill-Market Fit Reframe

People commonly confuse cause and effect when they tell others to follow their passion. A practical method involves mastering useful skills which leads to passion development naturally.

Instructions: This exercise? It helps you find out what you can market instead of what you like.

AI Prompt:

> Forget passion for a sec. I want to build a business based on skills. Help me out:
>
> 1 Pinpoint 5 skills that I already possess or that I could readily have based on [your field/experience].
>
> 2 Rank these skills based on:
> ∘ Market demand (high, medium, low)
> ∘ Competition (packed/okay/empty).
> ∘ My current proficiency. Expert? Competent? Beginner?
> ∘ Potential for growth? Future-proof?
>
> 3 For my top two skills, give me:
> ∘ Three real problems these skills solve for paying customers.
> ∘ Evidence. People willing to pay?
> ∘ A mastery roadmap. Showing how I could become exceptionally good at this
>
> 4 Suggest how I might develop genuine interest in this skill area even if I'm not initially passionate about it

Part 4: The Courage Connection

Let's be brutally honest. Fear—not lack of skill—kills most business dreams. ***Fear is the passion-killer.*** Let's stare it down.

Time to Get Real:
Skills and opportunity are useless without guts.
Use this prompt, filling in your business idea.
AI Prompt:

> Using my business concept [describe your concept], assist me with:
>   1 Identify my 3 biggest fears.
>   2 Find 5 examples of similar people succeeding.
>   3 Create a "permission slip" statement that acknowledges both my fears and the evidence against them (a self-pep-talk).
>   4 Create a simple 'courage ritual' I can do to get myself past the point of wanting to quit

Part 5: The Cathedral Perspective

And sometimes meaning in work can come from something other than passion: meaning can come from purpose. Reframing your business idea beyond self gratification is what this exercise helps with.
Reframing Time:
Use this prompt to give your business idea some serious purpose.
AI Prompt:

> Help me to see my business idea from the perspective of the '**cathedral builder**'.
>   1 Specifying 3 ways my business could genuinely help others or serve a greater cause
>   2 Framing statements (3 different ones to attach work to something greater than work)
>   3 Examples of businesses where people in my space took business that was 'cutting stone' and turned it to 'building cathedrals '. Provide specific company names.
>   4 Suggesting how I might measure impact beyond profit that would give me satisfaction even when the work is difficult (what metrics matter besides the bottom line?).

This activity: passion meets skills meets market meets meaning. Not about chasing unicorns. You must locate where your expertise meets the marketable issues and meaningful tasks which you enjoy working on even when putting in endless hours. *It's building your cathedral.*

ACTIVITY: THE AI IDEA ACCELERATION LAB

Many of the most successful businesses today came as 'happy accidents'. Think *Post-it Notes*. Or *Play-Doh*. The purpose of this lab is to engineer those accidents.

This isn't the college roommate's brainstorming session. We're looking for business ideas that *Google* search engine can't give you on page 37. AI will use its pattern recognition and your human intuition.

Do these phases in order.

Phase 1. *Divergent Explosion. Quantity Over Quality.*

Instructions: Fire up three separate AI chats. Different angles. Different vibes.

Chat 1: *The Niche Assassin*

AI Prompt:

> What I am passionate about is [your passion area]. Within this space, generate 25 highly specific sub niches. These must meet these criteria:
>   1.   Have online communities that are practically rabid with passion.
>   2.   Contains specific problems people would pay to solve
>   3.   Include at least 5 niches that are totally off my radar.
>   4.   Each has a twist sharper than a sushi chef's knife
>
> For each niche, provide:
>   - The specific audience segment
>   - Their primary pain point
>   - A potential solution format. Product/service/content.

Chat 2: *The Mad Scientist*
AI Prompt:

> These 10 unrelated industries can help me find unexpected business opportunities when [your passion/skill] is combined with them.
>   1. Sustainability
>   2. Education
>   3. Mental health
>   4. Fitness
>   5. Finance
>   6. Entertainment
>   7. Home improvement
>   8. Pets
>   9. Travel
>   10. Technology
>
> Provide. For each combination.
>   - Specific problem this hybrid may solve
>   - The unique thing about this opportunity
>   - Why the conventional ways have not been effective.

. . .

Conversation 3: *The Trend Surfer*

For the following prompt it is preferable to use a model that has access to the Internet and has deep research and reasoning capabilities. Monica, Perplexity, OpenAI...

AI Prompt:

> Select 15 emerging trends, technologies or cultural shifts which may provide business opportunity in the space of [your interest area] during next 3 to 5 years.

For each trend:
  1. Explain why this creates a market gap
  2. Describe 2-3 specific business ideas that leverage this trend
  3. Suggest why early movers would have an advantage
  4. Who will be the competition eventually? (Name names or types.)

Phase 2: *Idea Matrix. Synthesis.*

Now create a fourth conversation to bring together the most promising elements from your previous sessions.

AI Prompt:

> Idea overload. Help. TOO MANY IDEAS. Find the best—the gold nuggets—best combos only. Create an idea Synthesis Matrix with the following Ingredients.

FROM PREVIOUS SESSIONS:
  - My top 3 niches: [X, Y, Z]. From chat 1.
  - Top 3 cross-industry mutants: [A, B, C] from chat 2
  - Top 3 trends: [1, 2, 3] from chat 3

Make a 3x3x3 matrix of how each niche can pair with each cross industry idea and each trend. For the 5 most promising combinations, provide:
  1. A concise business concept name and description
  2. Why is this combo unique?
  3. The primary customer segment and their key problem
  4. What makes this difficult for others to replicate
  5. 'Weirdness score' (1-10). How unusual is this?

P hase 3: *The "Yes, And..." Expansion Workshop*

Pick your top 2 matrix ideas—the chosen ones—the finalists.

AI Prompt:

Improv technique "Yes, And" can be applied to the development of this business concept: [insert your idea].

For each of the following components respond, 'Yes, and...' to expand the concept:
1. Yes. This solves [primary problem] and could solve also...
2. Yes, [target audience] would value this, and we could also attract...
3. Yes. We could monetize through [obvious method], and we could also...
4. Yes. We could certainly market this through obvious channel, and we could also...
5. Yes, this can begin at [initial format] and become...

Now kill 90% of these expansions. After this "Yes, And..." frenzy, pinpoint the 3 expansions that turn the original idea into something truly next-level valuable and unique.

ACTIVITY: AI COLLISION CHAMBER – UNEXPECTED IDEAS THAT BECOME PROFIT POTENTIAL

Your 18th century poetry obsession? **Could pay the bills?** Well, let's find out.

Forget theory. **Brainwaves become bucks** in this activity.

S **uccessful businesses** today began their journeys following *major business model changes*.

- YouTube began as a video dating site.
- Shopify started as a snowboard equipment store before becoming an e-commerce platform.
- Twitter started as a podcast subscription platform called *Odeo*.

The common thread? Business owners knew how to transition from their initial dreams into serviceable business ideas.

A **business model reality check** allows you to maintain your passion while finding the most sustainable version of it that will succeed in the market. The hard part however is to be honest about what drives you and what the actual market need is.

. . .

Part 1: *The Passion-Problem Collision*

So what we will do first is to create what I call a *'collision chamber'*. Your interests will be merged with real world problems people have.

Step 1: Use AI. Create the two lists.
• List A: Your interests – at least 5.
• List B: Problems people face, at least 5.
AI Prompt 1: *Interest and Problem Lists.*

> I want to make two lists for a business brainstorming exercise:
> List A. List five questions to ask me. I am going to learn what I'm good at. Make them insightful.
> List B. Based on my answers, suggest 5 big problems that link to my interests—surprisingly. Don't be obvious.
> For each issue presented in List B, do note:
> • Who exactly suffers from this issue?
> • Why current fixes fail?
> • A surprising insight about this problem

Part 2: *The Idea Mixer*

Step 2: AI combines both lists. Mix List A and B—unexpectedly.
AI Prompt 2: *Business Idea Generator.*

> Using interests from List A: [insert your interests]
> And problems from List B: [insert problems]
> Create five ideas for business. Marry elements from the above. Randomly.
> • Give it a catchy name
> • One-sentence concept?
> • What is the unexpected problem solved?
> • Who would you determine would be most excited about this solution?
> • Propose one way to automate or improve that business idea. Using AI
> ***NO BORING IDEAS!***

Part 3: *The Challenge Round*

Step 3. Argue with it. With the AI.
Pick one concept among the ones you like so far.
AI Prompt Template:

CONCEPT 1. [PASTE IT HERE]

Act as a skeptical venture capitalist. Criticize. Analyze. Be harsh. *Devil's advocate mode:*

• Argue that my idea will fail. Justify.

• Name 3 different types of groups who will vigorously resist and oppose it. Who are the naysayers?

• Pointing out 3 practical roadblocks

Now switch perspectives. Become the idea's champion. Fend off your comments and defend the idea. Fight back logically.

One by one argue against each remark to the point of submission.

Got any ideas for a shift? How should we change?

State the "hidden gold" in this idea that the critics are missing completely.

Now assist me in strengthening the idea by:

• Resolving the issues

• Changing direction

• Providing one low risk strategy to test the concept

[*Rinse and repeat. For concept 2 and 3.*]

Part 4. *Fast Fails Big Wins.*

Instructions. Evolve one concept through quick iterations. *Fast failure is your friend here. Seriously.*

Prompt to launch iteration mode:

AI Prompt 4. *Quick Iteration Simulation.*

So let us iterate on the business concept which you have already selected from our previous work before going forward. Fast.

Let's imagine we are executing this out in real life, and we need to come up with 5 sequential iterations:

ITERATION 1. Initial concept

• Key hypothesis.

• What did we learn?

• What breaks or doesn't work

ITERATION 2. Feedback. Change of direction

• What we changed and why

• New hypothesis

• What we learn.

[Continue this process toward Iteration 5.]

5 iterations in? Analyze. Sum up:

• Which parts from Iteration 5 differ from Iteration 1? Trace the evolution.

• Which change helped most?

• What did we learn regarding the market need? Be specific.
• Anything unpredictable?

Part 5: *The One-Page Business Concept*
Alright. Business strategy time.
AI Prompt 5: *One-Page Business Concept Document.*

Based on all our discussion, help me create a one-page business concept for:
[Paste your final idea]
Include:
• Killer headline?
• The core problem this solves (1-2 sentences)
• My unique solution approach (2-3 sentences)
• The people we're targeting. Who are we serving?
• The tech. The specific applications. AI applications.
• How will it make money?
• How will you test this? Three simple steps
• Make this look nice as a one page document I can refer to later.

Image Generation Prompt (for your logo):

Create a simple logo for my business **YOUR BUSINESS NAME**. Focuses on **YOUR BUSINESS FOCUS**. Audience is **YOUR AUDIENCE**. Modern style. Clean. Pro. Colors. Simple Icon.

This whole process? *It's repeatable.* Need more ideas? *Run it again.* Would you like to research a fresh market direction? *Run it again.*

ACTIVITY: THE PROBLEM-TREND GOLD MINE EXPEDITION

To know what to do, know first what not to do.

This activity refines your idea. It's *not* about starting over. It's about digging deeper. *Inversion thinking* allows you to see blind spots. It helps you innovate.

Phase 1. *The Deeper Problems*
Instructions: The purpose of this phase is to refine your initial concept to find specific problems in a selected area. The activity dives deeper into established ground rather than restarting from the beginning.

For standard offline assistants use the below prompt but add the following in the beginning of the prompt.

"First—*data dump request*. Tell me. What do you need to map this market? To to properly analyze this market like:
  • Subreddits? Forums? Online dens of discontent where people complain? List them all.
     • Types of search trend data that would be valuable
     • Other data sources I could explore manually"

Then, after providing any available data, use the prompt below.

Alternative AI Prompt (For models with web search capabilities - *Monica, Merlin, Perplexity, NinjaChat, etc.*):

I already have an initial business concept in [*describe your concept*]. Help me to go deeper into those specific problems it addresses by utilizing your web search and analysis capabilities.
  Research and analyze:
  1 Identify 7 specific sub-problems within my concept area that people are actively struggling with according to recent online discussions (include direct evidence from forums, social media, etc.)
  2 I need the following.
  ◦ The exact user segment experiencing this problem (age, occupation, situation, etc.)
  ◦ Limitations of the solutions people are currently trying.
  ◦ How people describe this problem in emotional language. Quote their rage/frustration/despair. Give me the emotional temperature.
  ◦ One surprising insight. Something unexpected about each problem. Blow my mind.
  3 Now, rank these problems. Consider the following.
  ◦ Urgency (the actual urgency of the problems being solved at that moment)
  ◦ For some, explosions in frequency of mentions, being shouted about the loudest.
  ◦ Something actually worth solving—or maybe even better, solid indication that people have a certain willingness to pay to get it solved.
  4 Finally, pinpoint two or three problems that are clearly on the upswing—frequency spiking in the last six to twelve months. Show me the trend lines.

Phase 2: *Trend Refinement*

Instructions: General trends are interesting. ***Microtrends*** are the focused power surges.

For standard offline assistants use the below prompt but add the following in the beginning of the prompt.

> " First you tell me what trend data would be necessary for doing a complete analysis?
> • Specific industry reports that would be valuable
> • Data sources for consumer behavior shifts in this area
> • Tech adoption metrics that would be relevant
> After I provide any available data, help me identify:"

Then Provide what you can and use this prompt.

Alternative AI Prompt (For models with web search capabilities):

> I want to refine my understanding of trends specifically related to my concept in [*your concept area*]. Use your web-eyes to find current trend data.
> **Research.**
> 1 5 emerging microtrends directly relevant to my concept, including evidence.
> ○ Recent industry report and analysis (last 6 months).
> ○ Investing evidence
> ○ The trend data of search interest growing
> 2 For the microtrends I also need the following.
> ○ Evidence of its current position when it comes to adoption
> ○ Expert opinions
> ○ Available research to draw out demographics that are driving adoption.
> 3 Establish a diagram that demonstrates potential combination scenarios of microtrends for amplified market opportunities.
> 4 After performing comprehensive research identify the one trend that demonstrates maximum potential. The one with the strongest evidence of: early growth, the ability to scale big, and a direct line to those validated problems we found in Phase 1.

Phase 3: *The Inversion Thinking Workshop*
Master failure to master success.

Instructions: First, let's utilize the powerful reverse engineering technique of *inversion thinking* to clarify what we do not want to do.

AI Prompt:

I will make use of the *inversion thinking* technique to understand my concept clearly. Rather than directly coming up with ideas for how to succeed, we'll start by defining how to completely fail, and then inverting them.

The following is my concept. [*PASTE IT HERE*]

1 Help me brainstorm ten—ten guaranteed methods to faceplant. How to completely self-destruct? I mean epic failure.

◦ What features of the product/service would ensure no one would want it?

◦ Customer experience. Make it frustrating?

◦ What business model blunders would be a profit black hole?

◦ What marketing moves would make us invisible to the entire planet?

◦ Mistakes of the team that kill the project.

2 Now, invert each failure mode into a success principle:

◦ Identify the opposite approach for each "guaranteed failure"

◦ Explain why this inverted principle leads to success

◦ Who is succeeding by inverting common mistakes? Like real companies...

3 One counterintuitive insight. Something I wouldn't find by thinking positively.

Phase 4: *The Solution Inversion Workshop*

Instructions: Apply *inversion thinking* to solutions.

AI Prompt:

It's time to use inversion to compose killer solutions. Take those top three problems we unearthed in Phase 1. We should turn these problems around to create effective solutions.

PROBLEM 1: [*Insert refined problem from Phase 1*]

1 Listing how this problem is typically solved today

2 Identifying 3 assumptions these solutions make

3 List 5 ways to completely invert the approach

4 For each inversion, develop a specific solution concept that embodies this inverted thinking

5 Explaining how AI could make each inverted solution possible

[Repeat this same process for Problems 2 and 3—just copy and paste and swap out the problem.]

Which inverted solution is best? Consider:

• Better user experience.

• Does it ride the trend wave identified in Phase 2?

• With current tech. Is it feasible?

Phase 5. *Trend Amplification*

Instructions. Your newly refined solution. We'll position it to ride and amplify the trends that are the most promising.

AI Prompt:

> AI trend amplifiers, final mission. Use my refined solution [*your inverted solution*] as the product you help me position to best align with our most promising trend we identified [*key trend from Phase 2*]. You should create a "*Trend Amplification Strategy*" which consists of:
>
>   1 Trend Integration Roadmap:
>   ° Integrate trend elements into the product.
>   ° Three features leveraging the trend.
>   ° 12-month vision.
>   2 Trend Positioning Strategy:
>   ° Signal to early adopters.
>   ° 5 elements of messaging that should be included in marketing.
>   ° Which platforms?
>   3 Multi-Trend Advantage:
>   ° 2 additional trends to incorporate for more impact
>   ° Unique positioning.
>   I also need a one paragraph pitch. Nail it. Solution + trends + problems = irresistible offer.

Bonus. Image Prompt.

> [*Solution*] used by a group of beginners. A playful and optimistic illustration. Also 'lightbulb moment' style and bright colours to emphasize 'innovation'."

(You can later use this image in your business plan or product page!)

ACTIVITY: *IDEA VALIDATION WORKSHOP*

This gives you clarity. This whole process is designed to be tough. This activity forces you to thoroughly validate your business idea through multiple lenses, just as Edison would have done before investing his time and resources. It tests your idea thoroughly. *It is far better to kill a flawed idea early.* Good luck.

. . .

The Idea Interrogation Framework

Instructions: First, thoroughly document your idea for the AI to effectively analyze it.

AI Prompt:

I need a brutally honest evaluation of this business idea. No sugarcoating. Be my "No-BS Idea Validator." Honesty is your only hope here.

MY IDEA [PASTE it here]

I wanted to share some additional context that will help you to properly evaluate this.

Who's paying? [Your ideal customers]

What's the actual problem? [The pain point]

My fix? [Your solution]

Why me? [Your unique angle]

Cash plan? [Revenue model]

My credentials? [Your skills]

What I've got? [Resources]

Start first by reflecting this idea back to me, with respect to any inconsistencies, points of ambivalence, or the state of assumptions that need to be clarified before attempting to validate.

The Four Interrogators Analysis

Instructions: Now put your idea through the four critical validation questions mentioned in the text.

AI Prompt:

Through the lens of "The Four Interrogators of Viability," analyze my business idea.

INTERROGATOR 1. WHO'S DESPERATE FOR THIS? Find 3-5 particular type of customer who would need this solution The desperation level of each segment should be rated from 1 to 10 because desperate customers buy while indifferent ones do not. What proof exists that these target individuals genuinely want this solution? Which customer group would demonstrate the highest level of desperation for my solution? Describe them in detail I need to identify unexpected customer segments which I might have missed.

INTERROGATOR 2. "IS THE PIE BIG OR CRUMBS?" The realistic market size for this specific idea is to be estimated. I want to know what data points explain whether this market is growing or shrinking. What is the saturation of this market? What is likely to be my realizable market share of this market? Am I targeting large enough market such that my financial goal will be supported?

INTERROGATOR 3. "WHO'S ALREADY EATING?" Find 3-5 direct and indirect competitors. What are the particulars of their strengths and weaknesses? How could I exploit the areas in their offerings which they lack? What would these competitors do if I entered the market? I should evaluate whether any unanticipated entry barriers exist in the market.

INTERROGATOR 4 ASKED "ARE YOU FINANCIALLY ABLE TO FIGHT THIS BATTLE?" What would be the actual expenses needed to launch this business concept? What would be the ongoing expense (not just the initial payment) that I would be looking at? How much time it could take for this to become profitable? Or What skills/resources do I lack and would be essential. Are there any expenses which I have not identified?

Chain of Thought: For each factor, show your work! Based on these four interrogations, provide an overall viability score (1-10) with specific reasoning.

The AI Shark Tank Simulation

Run a simulation where you present your idea to investors who will query you on tough subjects while testing your predictions.

AI Prompt:

Step into the role of 3 different investors acting in a Shark Tank type scenario.

INVESTOR 1: THE MARKET SKEPTIC The investor expresses doubt about whether your product/service will find enough customers to succeed.

INVESTOR 2. THE EXECUTION GUY This investor challenges your ability to properly execute on this idea with what you have available now.

INVESTOR 3: THE COMPETITIVE ANALYST The investor believes that market competition makes entry too difficult for your business. They might say the following. "Google just launched this feature yesterday. Now what?"

The investors should:

Ask me 2 specific difficult questions on my idea
    Identify a particular assumption which demonstrates potential weakness in my plan
    Suggest one specific area where I need more validation
    Then, provide guidance on the following. What market data do I need to answer these concerns? I need to design a simple experiment which will validate my fundamental assumptions. What factors would persuade these investors to change their doubtful attitude?

The AI-Enhanced SWOT Analysis

Now perform a detailed SWOT analysis combined with AI's data driven perspective.

AI Prompt:

Perform an AI-Enhanced SWOT Analysis for my business idea. Your feedback should avoid vague statements because you must provide targeted directions for real improvement:

STRENGTHS: Actual advantages. "Your FDA contacts let you fast-track trials" beats "Passionate team".

WEAKNESSES: I mean killers. "Requires $200k upfront manufacturing" is a weakness well defined as opposed to "Limited Instagram followers". Where are you personally the weak link?

OPPORTUNITIES: Ideas like "Gen Z's obsession with [X] is a perfect timing scenario for the bet..."

I must identify three suitable market opportunities that will become available for me to seize in their appropriate timeframe.

There are emerging trends that perfectly match my idea. I should identify three market segments that lack proper service. Anything tech related?

THREATS: Example. "California's pending law could ban your core feature by 2025" is an existential risk.

What 3 external threats could become derailments for this idea? Who among my competitors is likely to be the most aggressive? The business viability could be affected by upcoming economic and regulatory changes. If my solution is going to be obsolete at any point, what technology shift is going to be the cause?

Support each SWOT point with evidence.

Convert all business terminology into basic language while providing detailed explanations of complicated ideas at the level of someone who knows nothing about the subject.

The Go or No Go Decision

Instructions: Synthesize all the validation data. Go? No Go?
AI Prompt:

Using all the validation analysis we had, I need your help to make a data driven decision on my idea. Use the validated insights to create a practical recommendation.

VALIDATION SCORECARD: We need to summarize all major discoveries found during validity testing Use a scale of 1-10 to evaluate my idea. The problem validation stage determines whether the solution addresses genuine painful issues. Market validation addresses if the opportunity promises a substantial enough market size. Competitive analysis shows if an opportunity exists to provide effective competition. Resource validation determines whether I possess sufficient resources to achieve success.

DECISION PATHS: Based on these scores, recommend ONE of these paths with specific reasoning:

A) PROCEED: The validation around this idea is quite strong for all key metrics To wrap it up, outline 3 most important next steps. Determine which further validation steps would be necessary.

A) CHANGE DIRECTION: The concept has good merits but requires a serious change in the direction Suggest 3 directions Explain how each change of direction fixes up the weaknesses in the validation. The most promising direction should be recommended.

C) PASS: Fundamental flaws suggest this idea should be reconsidered Explain the deal-breakers Suggest 3 completely different ideas in adjacent spaces.

THE HARD TRUTH: The most critical validation insight to take away. Listen up. "Your idea's fatal flaw is [X]. Fix this or fold." Chain of Thought: For each factor, show your work!

The Edison Implementation Planner

Create an actionable plan for ideas that succeed in validation to start working on the "99% perspiration" aspect.

AI Prompt:

Idea survived validation? Against all odds. Congratulations. Now—the real marathon begins. Edison knew—genius is mostly sweat—and smart planning.

MINIMAL VIABLE PRODUCT (MVP): I need to develop the most basic version of this concept to test its market potential. The essential features need identification before deciding which features fall into the nice-to-have category. Focus—ruthlessly—on core value—nothing else. How quickly could this MVP be completed if I have the necessary resources?

VALIDATION EXPERIMENTS: Design three low-cost experiments to nail down those key assumptions.

30-60-90 DAY PLAN: Create a timeline. Key objectives and milestones will be defined for the first 30 days. Days 31-60. Next phase goals Days 61–90: Scaling activities if earlier phases are successful.

RESOURCE ALLOCATION: What is the best way to distribute my current time resources? I need to determine how to distribute my current budget resources. I need to identify essential skill gaps along with their solutions. This also presents an opportunity to answer, what partnerships or relationships need developing?

SUCCESS METRICS: The success of this idea depends on three to five particular metrics which need evaluation. What indicators will demonstrate excellent performance results? When would it be appropriate to change direction because the results remain unfavorable?

The document should present an executable timeline I can initiate tomorrow.

R eady for the next step?
  Head to the Day 6 Theory section!

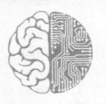

Day 6: Sleep While It Sweats.

Business Models. That Shouldn't Exist.

Here's the truth.
Building a scalable business does not require Stanford education or Silicon Valley investment capital. **Grit** combined with a solid idea and AI assistance will do the trick. You need to be gritty, have a good idea, and of course, you will require AI at your side.

Case Studies

Fernando Pessagno (aiCarousels)

Argentinian designer. Zero coding skills. **No Design Skills? No Problem.** Built a carousel generator in 10 days while streaming it live. And now? His AI tool is pulling in $5,000 every month. Recurring revenue. Five grand. Monthly. Think about that for a sec. **"I can't code" is an excuse. "I don't need to." is the reality now.**

Sabatino & Silke (Imagined with AI)

Freelancer + girlfriend duo. AI portraits on demand. Sold portraits within 24 hours. **First day!** Customers in 25+ countries. 234,000+ images generated. Annual income? $54,000. The side hustle? Outearns the 9 to 5. **They're doing it right.**

Adrian (Cleanvoice AI)

Ex-data scientist. Hated editing podcasts. So, naturally, he built Cleanvoice AI. It auto-edits podcasts. Bye-bye filler words. Sayonara stutters. Cleanvoice now pulls in

$400 MRR. **Moral?** Solve your own headaches. ***The aspirin? They will pay you for that.***

Intuition Robotics (ElliQ)

Intuition Robotics made *ElliQ*. *ElliQ* nags seniors to take meds, tells jokes, and cuts loneliness. *ElliQ* uses AI to have real conversations, gives health and wellness advice, and is basically a companion. No, it's not *Wall-E*. People love it. Smart tech for smart aging.

A Learning Platform. Big Name Healthcare Provider

Good use of AI learning by a big healthcare provider. Training for medical staff? Better. Personalized learning. Virtual practice for procedures. Training time cut by 30%. Knowledge retention up 50% The provider also saw a 20% improvement in patient care quality

AI—The Superpower Cheat Code

Why does this work?

- Automate the boring stuff. Like editing podcasts. See Cleanvoice AI.
- Build fast and fail faster. See aiCarousels and Imagined with AI.
- Invent what doesn't exist (*ElliQ's* companion AI)
- Democratization of expertise (Silke selling art without painting)
- No special skills needed (aiCarousels).

AI's just tech bros? **WRONG.** It's for the impatient, the underfunded, the hustler who is going to, 'I'll figure it out.'
The Bottom Line
AI isn't stealing jobs. *It's stealing excuses*. Your move. Now it is time to do the same.

Level up time. Now we get serious.

The future of business is *AI-driven* but the future of *AI* is ***human-led***—ponder that. It's real. Yesterday you brainstormed. Ideas flew. Maybe some wild ones. Napkins might have been harmed.

Now? ***Reality check.*** It is now time to **bin the business fossils**. We are not about old school. We are about ***AI power.*** Competitors will weep bitter tears.

There is a false belief that achieving success through online business demands continuous innovation.

Truth: Old models plus AI. It's knowing the basics. Add AI. ***Boom.***

Forget the hype. Digital gurus push novelty. They are wrong. Online wealth? It's not new. It's old ideas reborn. Think *vintage cars*. Timeless. Reliable. Upgrade them? Heads turn. *AI? Your upgrade.*

Success in online business depends on having **three core elements** for every winning venture.
- First—*why you?* Your value. What makes you different?
- Second—*who cares?* Target audience. Who needs you?
- Third—*how to give it?* Delivery. How do they get value?

O ld models work. *Affiliate marketing. Freelancing. E-commerce.* These form the foundation which billions of online currency depend on. But 2010 tactics fail now. *AI is your edge.* It spots gaps. It automates tasks. It finds hidden gold. You focus on big ideas.

Why old school wins? Online wealth is about reinvention. Both professionals and novices deal with identical problems of yesterday. Every online business faces identical battles no matter how many struggles they have previously endured. Too much noise online. Markets are packed. Time is always short. Well, same as today. Find people. Give value. Grow fast. What changed? **Tools.** The integration of AI technology converts diligent work into efficient work operations.

- Example — affiliate marketing 2.0. Imagine AI. It spots hot products now. It writes killer those sequences that convert. You sleep. AI works.
- Freelancing, for instance. Still about skills for cash. But AI? Total transformation. Finding clients? Proposal writing? Even upselling? AI rewrites the game. Automates bills. You create. Not chase paper.
- E-commerce evolved. AI? More than just product tips. It designs them. The majority of customer service operations is managed through chatbots.

AI—advantage—friction to fuel switch. Every model has a weak spot. AI? Not magic. Partner in solving problems. Let's look at problems.

Take the competition conundrum. Yes—market's packed. **AI is your edge.** Data power. Weeks of work—minutes now.

Take the time trap. No more spreadsheets. Yes to life. AI automates the grind.

Customer smarts. *Pictory.ai* turns research—hours—to videos—3 minutes. Actionable summaries.

Mindset upgrade time. At this point you must view yourself as *CRO* because you serve as the *chief robot officer.* Stop task work. Start smart work.

Online success opportunities are available to people who adopt AI systems. Don't chase trends. Classic models—strong. *AI? Your unfair advantage.*

THE NEW ECONOMIC MODEL

Forget side hustles. *AI rewrites the pay rules.* Work? *Not 9-to-5 anymore.* Passion for paychecks is outdated. AI fills the gap. Forget the corporate ladder. Your quirks become your bill payers. Below are three models making profit out of pajama time.

Passion Economy + Your Quirks

Knitting? Thimble collecting? Teaching cats to high-five? *You're CEO material.* AI boosts niche obsessions.

GPT is your roleplay buddy for audiences on demand. It identifies the very people who are interested in your vintage teapot course and spits out their pain points. Role-plays? It's good at it. Like scary good. Interview your market for free to find their needs? You bet! Creepy? Yes. But effective.

Scaling up feels impossible? Nope. One-on-one coaching? So old school. Evergreen courses with AI. *Seriously passive income.* Like, super passive. *Finally!*

Would balcony beekeeping be a good idea? AI Research Assistants can identify and validate upcoming trends before Google Trends begins its daily operations.

CREATOR ECONOMY: *GATEKEEPERS? WHAT ARE THOSE?*

TV deals? Nah, we're good. We've got the internet. Like *YouTube*. Like *Patreon*. Like *Substack*...

Brain Fog? **Solved:** Blank screen terror? With Rytr (or Jasper) you can generate blog outlines before the creative barriers appear in your mind.

AI tools are the trend predictors for your niche. You're first. Everyone else? Late.

Ebook price? AI decides—$9.99 or $49.

Grandpa? Tech god—50k TikTok subs. His simple smartphone and computer tips are something seniors dig. Descript edits his videos. TubeBuddy boosts his SEO. Grand-kids ask him for WiFi help.

SHARING ECONOMY MODEL

Your car sits parked. Your tools rust. Your guest room is a spider Airbnb. Time to mone-tize the clutter.

AI software dynamically prices kayak rentals. Rain? Festival? Prices shift. Like magic —but with algos.

Upwork uses matchmaker mode, that is, AI to match your knitting skills with the scarf–desperate soul. No resume needed. Skills speak louder anyway.

Trend Surfing: Christmas pet-sitting demand in July? AI sees it. You profit.

Retirement? Ha! Grandma thought she was done. Unretired. Now she teaches gardening. Online. The whole internet gardens with her. *Canva* designs ads. Her roses —and ROI—look great.

Why This Works Now:

AI manages repetitive work such as analytical tasks and search engine optimization and providing services. You bring unique human qualities which include your innova-tive thinking as well as determination and your special style of humor. Tools? Easy to get. Competition? Overrated. *Your unique spin? Priceless.*

And so, if you are set to transition to the next section, remember that the tools exist. The opportunities are ripe. The final ingredient is your uniquely **you** perspective whether as an early beginner or a senior in search of a second act.

MINDSET UPGRADE—AI EDITION

From Survival to Thrival

You're at a fork in the road. **Old way? Slow. New way? AI fast lane.** Old online grind — left path. Right path: AI power boost.

Remember *Blockbuster*? Movie rental giants—gone. *Netflix* arrived. Game over. They missed the *Netflix* boat. Their real mistake? Ignoring a huge change. Many thought that *Netflix* was the reason for *Blockbuster's* failure, but actually they missed a shift. They whiffed on the future, not for lack of cash. They had cash—but no clue. They missed the new wave.

The change now? **AI's power for everyone.** AI will not replace your business but will rather enhance your business operations. No matter how young or old you are, AI is your unfair edge. Use it to:

• Kill time-wasting tasks.
• Turn data into decisions.
• Personalize offers.
• Sort signal from BS.

Adapt or Die—Seriously

Imagine a tireless partner. Works 24/7. Never complains. That's AI on your team.

THE 4 AI SUPERPOWERS THAT ARE AVAILABLE FOR YOU RIGHT NOW.

Churning Content at Scale

An insightful claim by *HubSpot* is that businesses with 16 or more blog posts have 3.5x more traffic. Without burnout, AI is a way to speed up the path to those levels of traffic.

AI is a creative partner. Not for writing your content. Content builds trust. But it's hard to make. Articles that grab eyeballs. Video scripts that wow. AI writing tools? Time savers—yes. But also: **optimized, magnetic content.** Speak your audience's lingo. Without any writing skills (almost!), create a month's worth of content in just a matter of minutes.

Want a taste? What you should prompt AI with is this:

> **"Hello AI—your expertise in content marketing is beyond human capacity. Here's my business model. Here's my target audience. Need content for that biz. Three content ideas—three versions each."**

Example Business: affiliate marketing. The target is young adults who are not partial to ecology. Boom—AI ideas appear.

Mine Gold in "Boring" Niches

F inding gold niches used to be guesswork. Months of it. Hot niches? Not just lying around. You gotta dig. Real people. Real wallets. Zero competition. Enter your robot assistant.

Market research prompt:

> **"AI—market guru. Want an online biz—[your broad industry]. Find three hot, empty niches. Why are they goldmines?"**

Automate Like a Boss

Even beginners can streamline their business without coding.

Time is the ultimate non-renewable resource. Tools like *Zapier, ManyChat*? Your tireless 24/7 crew. Tasks you hate? Data entry? Social media schedules? These drain your soul. AI is your robot assistant. It loves boring stuff.

Imagine a busy working mom:

- Handmade soap-business automated
- *Klaviyo's* AI crafting cart recovery emails (Cha-ching!)
- *Pally* auto-scheduling *TikTok* posts during daycare hours
- "Where's my order?" queries that are being handled by *Zendesk* bots.

Personalize Like Amazon

Customers crave that YOU treatment. Generic marketing is basically invisible. AI, though? It shows exactly which 60-year-old wants yoga for arthritis vs. pickleball training. Casual lookers turn into buyers. Best part? AI does the boring stuff. You get to be clever.

The Playbook's in Your Hands

The only difference between your competitors and you is their speed of implementing artificial intelligence in their operations. We will connect these tools to your particular objectives in the upcoming section. But first—get this—your limits—age, newbie status, tight budget—gone. The real risk? Waiting until "someday".

Oh, and that upcoming Business Model Matchmaker exercise in the workbook section is not busywork. ***It's your actual blueprint.***

No experience? Even better. AI loves a clean slate.

FOLLOW YOUR PASSIONS?

'Follow your passion'? NOT a business myth. What do you think helps you keep on keeping on when problems and tribulations arise? That being said, passion is NOT set in stone. Passion can be developed through hard work. But hard work alone does not guarantee success to the extent that rowing hard does not guarantee staying afloat. Pick

boats instead of simply rowing with great effort. Many row hard—but go nowhere. People choose boats that will not lead them to their desired locations. They pick the wrong boats. Boats going the wrong way. Boats that sink.

Trends? Silly detours maybe. What really matters? ***Skills people pay for.*** Find those skills fast. Do this before the spark dies.

For example—jewelry.

Make jewelry you love. They say. Right boat evaluation asks whether customers wish to purchase the product. Do the residents in your area seek out necklaces that are similar to yours? What styles sell?

Necklace whiz and buyers around? ***Bingo—your boat!***

WHY BUSINESS MODELS MATTER?

Take two bakers. One sells sourdough at farmers' markets. The other ships gluten-free cookie mixes worldwide through Shopify. Both love baking, but their business models decide their freedom. Wrong model? Endless grind. Right one—self-sustaining.

Yet there are three traps:

- The first one is ***Analysis Paralysis***: Ever arguing "e commerce vs. SaaS vs. freelancing" in your head.
- Second, jumping on trendy models that are not a good fit. A retiree day trading NFTs? Rarely a fit unless they are also secretly garage mining.
- Third, underestimating hidden costs, skills or tools. Say, creating a viral TikTok campaign without first understanding Gen-Z's 'icks' or 'sigma' obsessions to feed the algorithm.

FROM GUESSWORK TO PRECISION

AI anticipates. It doesn't just analyze. AI penetrates beneath apparent patterns which we people usually focus on.

- ***Market Pulse***: Let's assume the general interest in shorter, snackable classes or courses is increasing, or maybe the interest in building an hour-long webinar is declining?
- ***Skill Audits***: Is there a requirement of one or multiple skills in remote sales that you do not possess? You may be guided to podcasting by AI.
- ***Scalability Sniff Tests***: Is this model going to need 4,800 hours a year or am I going to start getting paid for it while I am asleep?
- ***Risk DNA***: Sensitivity of risk models to your "sweat during a flip of a coin" personality. AI takes your nerves into account when it comes to risk.
- ***Risk Radar***: Love wild risks? Or panic at paper cuts? AI sees your fear level. It matches the plan to your guts. No more sweaty palms.

Imagine a senior assuming they need video skills to teach online. Wrong. AI rolls its digital eyes. "Dude, ditch the lights. Type like *Hemingway*. Words are your superpower." Tech headaches—AI's problem. Brilliance—yours.

STRATEGIC SURRENDER

The role of data is to elevate intuition.

While relying on your instinct is crucial you need to use data to eliminate your preconceived ideas. AI is not here for taking your place; it's what stops you from embracing comfort. You feel safe staying with coaching but AI data signaling you to transition to affiliate marketing because your network's 10X more valuable there. Maybe you go overboard. AI simplifies. Transform your 12-module program into an easy-to-purchase $17 package.

ANTI-FRAGILITY? AI HELPS WITH THAT AS WELL.

Forget vague pep talks. Three AI techniques can make your business immune to market threats:

- First, **The Constraint-First Filter.** You can ask AI for guidance about creating the most basic version of your idea which integrates with your scheduling limitations, financial resources and technological abilities. A busy mom who plans to start coaching begins by consulting AI for advice. AI delivers. Ditch Zoom calls. The solution includes voice notes coupled with a $27/month app. First test market demand before building the product. Boom!
- Second, **The Sunk Cost Killer.** AI uses existing assets such as your email list and social media following and past projects to discover ways of using these resources again instead of starting from zero. For instance: "You've already got 872 blog readers. Do not create an entire new course. Monetize them now with a 'Best Of' PDF and some AI-generated upsell offers."
- Third, **The Pre-Mortem Protocol.** Make AI simulate failure for your business model. Ask it: "Why would this TikTok shop fail within six months?" The answers become your plan B. For example, AI might say:
- "You'll burn out editing daily Reels—pre-record 50 templates now."
- "Your dropshipping profits will disappear." The solution? "Shift to affiliate reviews by the third quarter of the year."

What we are not trying to do is predict the future. Adaptability. Your business DNA. They need to merge.

The future is hybrid. It belongs to those who use AI's logical power to boost their own human strengths. Let competitors be stuck in "what if" scenarios. Use AI to:

- Really understand the risks. For example. AI analysis. Your "low-competition" niche is in fact a deserted market.

- Take advantage of trends. Example. AI identifies. The Substack algorithm recently began promoting controversial articles about AI issues.
- Create leverage. Example. One-click AI funnel upgrade. One-time clients become repeat customers.

Making piles of cash? Not the only goal here. Think about your life. Do you wish to be a slave to your work? No. Business is leverage. Not your boss. Let it fit your life. Like a good pair of jeans.

Everyone asks. Can AI do this? Sure, maybe. But the real question? AI can lift the heavy boxes. It can do the boring stuff. *So what will you do now? Build a castle? Paint the sky purple? Make something amazing. Go on, you've got help now.*

KEY TAKEAWAYS

- Know your *why*, *who*, and *how*. These are your business *holy trinity*. Now, *AI-power them*.
- *The Old + the new = GOLD*: Classic business models such as *affiliate, freelancing, e-commerce* are not over and done with. Old Models, New Power. Affiliate, freelance, e-commerce. Timeless. Now AI-charged.
- You are the *Chief Robot Officer*, do not waste time doing task work. Let AI sweat the small stuff. You think big. *Smart work wins*. Ditch the grind.
- *Passion for paychecks is outdated. Passion + quirks = profit.* Seriously. Passion + Quirks + AI. *Pajama Paydays*. Get paid for being YOU.
- *Gatekeepers are dead*. Long live *YouTube Grandpas*. AI turns anyone into a *creator king*.
- *Monetize EVERYTHING with AI.* Turn clutter into cash flow.
- *Blockbuster* failed because it ignored change. *Don't Blockbuster yourself.* AI is the new *Netflix*.
- Business is a *leverage*, not a *labor*. That leverage is provided by AI.
- Content. Niches. Automation. Personalization. AI provides the leverage for that.
- Skills that pay > passion. "Follow passion" is BS out of context. *Follow the money.*
- Pick your boat wisely. Wrong model? Prepare to sink. *Right business model = freedom.*
- A good way to leverage your intuition with AI backed data is *Strategic Surrender*. Don't just trust your gut. Trust AI's data-powered gut. It's smarter.
- Analysis paralysis? Trendy traps? Hidden costs? *AI's your consultant.*
- Risk? AI manages: Your business model is built considering your risk tolerance and is resilient to it.
- Anti-fragile biz? Built with AI. Find constraints, kill sunk costs, and simulate failure to prepare. *Future-proof yourself.*

- *Future is Hybrid.* Don't debate, dominate.
- AI grinds. The robot workforce handles all heavy tasks. You create. Go big. Team up. *Time to be amazing.*

Theory? For thinkers in towers. Action? That is us. We build empires—*AI empires.* Ready to get dirty? The *Workbook Section for Day 6* awaits. *Let's go.*

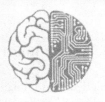

Day 6: WORKBOOK

Activity: The AI Business Model Transformer Workshop

"**The robots are coming!**" Is that a threat? Or an opportunity? I say *opportunity*. And not just any opportunity.

This activity walks you through reinventing traditional online business models with AI capabilities and positions yourself as a ***Chief Robot Officer*** such that you use AI for strategic purpose rather than to perform business activities.

Phase 1: *Business Model Archeology and Matchmaking*

Instructions: First **Identify**. Find the traditional online business model that aligns. **WITH YOU**. Think of this as business model dating.

AI Prompt:

> Work as my ***AI Business Model Matchmaker***. I need your help to find the most appropriate traditional online business models that match my particular circumstances.
>
> First, I'll share:
> • Skills: [Your top 3]
> • Passions: [Your obsessions]
> • Resources: [Time, cash, gear]
> • Income goals: [Be specific]
>
> Based on that glorious info—evaluate my match with these classic online biz models:
> • Affiliate Marketing
> • Freelancing/Service Provision

- E-commerce/Product Sales
- Content Creation
- Online Courses/Education
- Software/App Development
- Coaching/Consulting

For each model, provide:
- Score (out of 10) of its compatibility with my skills and interests.
- What do I have vs. what is required
- Realistic timeline to my income goals
- Key challenges I would likely face

Choose and explain why the top 3 most compatible models are great for my exact scenario

For my **#1** recommended model, provide a specific example of how someone with my background could implement it successfully

Phase 2: *The Three Core Elements Analysis*

Now, develop the three most important elements.
AI Prompt:

Help me to build the three basic components of my chosen business model: [PASTE IT HERE]

WHY ME? (My Unique Value Proposition)

From my background in [PASTE YOUR BACKGROUND]:

I need to identify five distinct methods through which I can separate my services from those of my competitors. Don't be a clone. Be a *unicorn* (a profitable one).
- 3 potential unique angles based on my specific experiences
- 2 combinations you would not expect. For my skills. That makes for a unique offering

From there, please assist me in writing a strong UVP statement to clearly communicate the various ways this offering is different and valuable to clients.

WHO CARES? (My Target Audience)

3-5 cohorts. That need my offering

For each segment, analyze:
- Pain points of theirs suited my solution
- Where they currently look for solutions. Forums? Social media? Carrier pigeons?
- What would make them choose me over alternatives
- Artificial Intelligence. How can it help me reach them.

Help me pick my main target audience. Then. Create an avatar.

HOW TO GIVE IT? (My Delivery Mechanism—The Goods)

Based on my business model, how am I actually gonna deliver this thing?

• 3-5 delivery formats. Also channels that would work best
• Pros and cons of each
• Artificial Intelligence. How can it improve each?

The combination that would deliver the most optimal customer experience

And recommend the optimal delivery approach that I should follow and how to implement them.

Phase 3: *The AI Enhancement Blueprint—Operation: Maximum Overdrive*

Instructions: Now identify the particular AI enhancements for your business model.

AI Prompt:

I need to develop an *AI Enhancement Blueprint* for the business model I selected. Detailed plan of how AI can change each critical function.

• **MARKET RESEARCH**
   ◦ What data can AI analyze?
   ◦ Which patterns can it recognize that I wouldn't recognize?
   ◦ Best AI tools or prompts?
   ◦ What would be the resulting benefit for me that affords me a competitive advantage?

• **CONTENT & OFFER CREATION**—*AI creativity booster.*
   ◦ What can be improved of my creation process?
   ◦ What can AI enable me to make more valuable, better, faster offers for people?
   ◦ What stays human-driven? What's AI-assisted?
   ◦ Best AI tools for this?

• **CUSTOMER ACQUISITION**—*Magnet Mode: On*
   ◦ Is there ever a situation in which AI can help with my marketing efforts?
   ◦ Which of the customer acquisition tasks can be handled with AI?
   ◦ Best AI tools for this?

• **SERVICE DELIVERY & OPERATIONS**
   ◦ AI has the ability to eliminate which operational bottlenecks from business operations?
   ◦ Through which methods does Artificial Intelligence enhance the experience of my customers?
   ◦ Which regular operations should I hand over to AI right now?
   ◦ I need to identify particular AI tools that will optimize these operational procedures.

• SCALING & OPTIMIZATION

◦ Which AI capabilities will assist me in recognizing new chances to grow my business?

◦ Which obstacles during scaling do AI technologies offer help in overcoming?

◦ Best AI tools for scaling?

For each area, give me:

• A *"Before AI vs. After AI"* comparison. Show me the transformation.

• Why this enhancement provides me a competitive advantage

• Specific prompts or workflows I can use immediately.

ACTIVITY: QUIRCK TO CASH

 "I have a hobby of collecting belly button lint. Is this weird?" - *Anonymous Redditor.*

Answer: Maybe. But it could be profitable.

Did you know that the average American has at least three marketable skills they completely undervalue? **THEY DON'T.** I just made this up. But you get the point.

Let's play *Quirk to Cash*.

First pick a *"Hidden Asset."* It is something you didn't consider to be a big deal. Choose one of these:

Category One: Dust Collectors.

A Rarely Used Physical Object: Be specific. Examples: A vintage camera. A specialized kitchen tool. What exactly is gathering dust?

Category Two: Secret Skills.

Skill you have. Seems normal to you. Are you a good listener? Can you fix anything? Master of folding fitted sheets. Don't laugh. These count.

Category 3. Weird addictions.

Some interests that are a little on the edge side. The ones that bring up the *no money here* signal. Knowing all 80s pop song lyrics. Obsessed with pigeons?

Got your Hidden Asset? Good. Write it down. Make it real.

Copy this exact prompt. Also, paste into any AI tool of your choice.

Get ready to see the actual monetary value of your interests that people consider useless.

 You are *Quirk Monetization King*. With AI. Weirdness needs to be turned into wealth. They come to you. They get a chance to find money concealed in their quirks.

YOUR HIDDEN ASSET can be monetized by AI? That's what I'd like to find out. Assume I know nothing about online business. Use these three money blueprints:

- **PASSION ECONOMY Riches:**
  ◦ Identify a surprising micro-audience desperate for content/products related to this quirk
  ◦ Come up with the design for the digital thing that they will buy. A guide? A course? A cheat sheet? Make it specific.
  ◦ *Artificial Intelligence hacks.* It can be built fast. No more trading time for dollars.
- **CREATOR ECONOMY Fame (and Fortune):**
  ◦ Identify an overlooked content format perfectly suited for this quirk (video style, article type, etc.) Not "social media posts". But TikTok ASMR videos.
  ◦ Describe a content series that would attract followers.
  ◦ *Artificial Intelligence?* Describe how this can really take a weight off when content creation comes into play.
- **SHARING ECONOMY**
  ◦ Find an unexpected asset or knowledge about this quirk that others would pay to access
  ◦ Suggest at least 3 ways I could rent it out. Or share access to it. Or offer related services to others.
  For the single best opportunity:
  • Provide a specific name/brand concept
  • First 3 steps to launch by Friday (Example: "1. Use *Midjourney* to create retro poster art 2. Set up a *Calendly* trial slot 3. Record a *Loom* demo video")
  • Explain why most people overlook this opportunity (the hidden insight)
  Get into the nitty-gritty. Skip the broad strokes. Your feedback should force my reaction to be *'I cannot believe I missed this insight.'*

When the AI spits out ideas:
Think Deeply:
Read the AI's suggestions carefully. Read it for real.

- What ideas surprise you most? Do that.
- Which tool suggestions are new to you?
- What is the best test you could run for $0 in 2 hours? It's overcomplication if you need a business license for your idea.

Final Boss Move: The "achievable" idea is usually the golden one.
"But what if I fail?" Cool. You will fail faster than a person who is 'still researching' their side hustle.

AI TIME MACHINE

In 1998, **Kodak** employed 170,000 people and sold 85% of the photo paper worldwide? Their business model faced complete destruction within several years. Digital photography eliminated their business model which resulted in major financial losses. Ouch. The kicker is this, however—*they invented the digital camera*. **Double ouch.**

What you have already seen is how AI converts challenges into new opportunities. Now, change your thinking. AI is powerful. Yes. But that's not the point. It is your view of its use in your life.

85% of jobs that will be available in 2030 do not yet exist? (Source: Dell Technologies and Institute for the Future). Let that sink in. Now, let's prepare.

Forget perfect predictions. Think ***strategic anticipation***. The concept is *"future-proofing"* your mind and business ideas. In order to see disruptions, we will use AI. AI finds trouble—then the gold inside.

The Activity Steps:
Industry Brainstorm

To begin with, jot down 3–5 industries or areas which you are genuinely interested in. They could be broad like *'health and wellness'*, *'education'*, *'creative arts'* or more specific *'carnivore diet'*, *'online tutoring for seniors'* and *'handmade jewelry'*. Do not overthink it, just list whatever pops up your curiosity.

Example (for the reader):
• Health and Wellness
• Personal Finance
• Travel

The "*Disruption Scenario*" Prompt (*AI Enters the Chat*)

Time to bring in the AI. What we're going to do is to use it to see how these industries might be flipped on their face within the next 5 10 years. The information aims to prepare you rather than frighten you.

This will be used with your favorite tool as the prompt for Text Generation.

> Role. Futurist mode—trend expert. I am interested in the following industry: [Insert Industry from Step 1]. 3-5 AI disaster scenarios—next 5-10 years. Wild but real. Business impact—consumer impact. For each scenario—also briefly suggest 1-2 potential NEW opportunities that could arise for entrepreneurs as a result of this disruption.

Reader Instructions: Copy—paste—fill in your industry. Run this prompt for each of your industries, one at a time. Read AI's answers. The hidden opportunities are there.

Opportunity Extraction:

The AI had disruptions and there were openings. Now, dig deeper. Ask yourself. For each scenario.

• What skills will be valuable? *Example*. Basic customer service can already be handled by AI. So, humans will need strong emotional intelligence.

- What fresh products will satisfy anticipated market needs?
- What skills can I reuse?

For each situation, write your answers. Details are key. *"Aha!"* moments incoming—fast.

"BLOCKBUSTER VS. NETFLIX":

Remember **Blockbuster**? Blockbuster choked because they were stuck on what they were losing—video rentals. They completely missed what they could gain—streaming. Revisit the notes you wrote during the last phase of analysis. The way you approach this situation resembles Blockbuster or do you take a Netflix perspective? **Be honest.**

An optional text-generation prompt extends the reflection process:

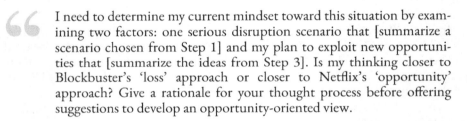

> I need to determine my current mindset toward this situation by examining two factors: one serious disruption scenario that [summarize a scenario chosen from Step 1] and my plan to exploit new opportunities that [summarize the ideas from Step 3]. Is my thinking closer to Blockbuster's 'loss' approach or closer to Netflix's 'opportunity' approach? Give a rationale for your thought process before offering suggestions to develop an opportunity-oriented view.

Reader Instructions: Honesty hour. Feeling stuck? Use the prompt. Get AI's view. Shift to potential gains.

Pick the idea that *electrifies* you.

A ctivity

THIS IS THE HYDRA HEAD CHALLENGE.

You Have to Grow Two New Wins for Each Problem

> *"The obstacle is the way."* — *Marcus Aurelius, Meditations.*

Ever heard that one? Let's upgrade that. Think **Hydra**. Mythical beast. Cut off one head—two grow back. That's the level. ***Resilience on steroids***. Market shifts? Problems? Fuel for your fire.

We have spent time discussing business models together with antifragility concepts. Bounce back is far too weak; let's go for something more. Just as in the myth of the Hydra: cut off one head and two grow back. That is the level of resilience and explosive growth we desire. Your business must be designed to prosper from every challenge and market shift alongside all unexpected problems rather than prevent risks altogether.

This activity is based on an amazing **AI Driven** technique to turn possible stressors into opportunities for exponential growth. Your business should consume unpredictability to become more powerful.

Instructions: *Hydra Business Builder*

1 Refine Your Business Idea: Based on the previous activities, solidify your chosen business model. Be very specific. Don't say "online coaching." Instead: *"$97/month membership. Weekly group coaching. Downloadable resources on procrastination for freelance writers. Free email newsletter and paid Facebook ads are how they market it."* Specificity is your first weapon.

2 Okay. Prepare for a brainstorm session and make a list of possible barriers to your business. Don't sugarcoat it. List 3 to 5 real-deal stressors. Seriously consider:

- **Market Meltdown:** New rival undercuts you? Niche market—gone tomorrow? Demand disappears?
- **Operations meltdown?** Tech implodes? Creation of content suddenly becomes a blackhole of time?
- **Money pit?** Ad campaigns tank? And then, payment processor will ghost you?
- **Personal implosion?** Burnout hits like a truck? And life throws you a sizable curveball, all of a sudden you are time poor.

3 List Your Constraints:

- **Time?** There are only 10 hours per week that I can give myself to.
- **Money?** My starting budget is $500.
- **Tech Skills?** I code like a toddler.
- **Other:** [Describe other limits]. My cat demands 3PM meetings

4 AI Prompt: Copy and paste the prompt below into the AI tool or two of your preference.

My venture revolves around creating an online business using this exact model: [Elaborate the business model further based on Step 1 modifications].

I want to design this business to be the mythical Hydra — when faced with a challenge ('head' being cut off), the business does not just recover, but in fact gets stronger, via the spawn of many new opportunities ('heads' growing back two at a time).

Here are my business stressors. Bring on the pain:

[Stressor 1: Detail the challenge. Example: 'Sudden economic downturn shrinks customer budgets.']

[Stressor 2: Detail the challenge]

[Stressor 3: Describe the challenge in detail – "Facebook bans my ad account"]

[More stressors? Add them.]
My sad constraints are:
Time: [Number] hours/week. Tick-tock.
Money: $[Dollar Amount]. Pennies.
Tech Skills. [Your level]
Other Limits: [Your limits]. Example: 'No prior experience in the coaching industry'.

Hydra Strategist mode—engage. Handle every stress factor without avoidance because it represents an opportunity for growth. Give me two ways each stressor becomes growth. Exponential growth. Big improvement. Think wild.

Consider:
Better Product? Force innovation? Upgrade? New features?

New Revenue? Different markets? Untapped customers? Expand horizons?

Stronger Brand? Community builder? Loyalty explosion? Deepen connections?

New Skills? Partnerships? Collaborate to conquer? Team up?

How to use constraints for advantage? Limits breed creativity? Turn weakness to strength?

Specific. Creative. Actionable. Hydra growth plans. Suppose that I take up the challenge, rather than being afraid of it."

5 Analyze and Prioritize:

- The AI will generate opportunities. Review the suggestions.
- Find the "golden heads": Find the most exciting, feasible, and 'golden' opportunities closely matching to your long term vision. Which are the ones that provide you with that 'dopamine rush'?
- Choose at least one 'Hyrda Head' strategy for each stressor that you will actively plan for. This has nothing to do with awaiting the stressor to occur; this is instead about having the ability to thrive in the event that it does.
- Implement the "Hydra Head" strategies directly into your main business strategy. Contingency plans—ready. New products—pipeline filling. Partnerships—on the horizon.

(Optional Image Generation Prompt)
For fun: Use this prompt in your AI image generator – *Flux, DALL-E, Midjourney, Stable Diffusion*, whatever you fancy:

"Make a striking image visually that will have some playfulness to represent 'Hydra-Growth Engine for an Online Business'. Feature a stylized friendly multi-headed Hydra in the image that presents a professional business-minded appearance without being frightening alongside digital symbols for online business expansion intertwined with plant or technological elements. The visual presentation needs optimism and inspiration to depict business resilience along with various opportunities for achievement."

I have generated one here with Flux on Monica.

Next Up: *Niche Power.*
Forget just surviving. You're a *Hydra* now. Weakness? **Growth trigger**. Most businesses dodge problems. You? You eat them for breakfast. Let's zero in on your niche.

R eady for the next step?
Head to the Day 7 Theory section!

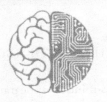

Day 7: RED OCEAN / BLUE OCEAN / YOUR OCEAN

Phantom Markets. Don't Google This.

O kay. Workbook session was productive. You have nailed this new revolutionary AI business model now. Awesome. But hold on. Before launching your plan we need to discuss how you will find your specific market group or tribe.

I am using ***tribe*** in this context to refer to your specific *target audience* rather than a drum circle gathering group. I'm talking about your *niche*. The exact audience which will genuinely embrace your product offering.

Today? ***Sherlock Holmes*** time. You need to invest your energy here because choosing a correct niche? ***Critical.*** As ever,

> ***"The riches are in the niches."***

Ever heard that one? It's a classic for a reason.

Want to cash in on AI? ***Niche down.*** Seriously.

Marketing "AI magic" to customers across the entire spectrum does not work. Using a goldfish net to catch a whale. Pointless, right? Niches are where it's at. Why? Because niches get you paid. Plain and simple. The key to success is to choose one specific field then direct your full power toward it and profits will start coming in. You can achieve financial success when you specialize in activities which truly motivate you.

Ok. First things first. Remind yourself about that AI business model which you had previously gotten excited about. Time to get specific.

Digital Products? Fantastic.

Forget generic Make Money Online courses. Dead on arrival. Nobody cares. Instead – think sharp. Teach accountants how to "Make Money Online" with "AI for Financial Forecasting." ***Boom.*** Or YouTubers? Teach YouTube creators the process of earning income with AI-based video editing. ***Boom***—target audience identified. See the difference?

Affiliate Marketing? Cool.

Promoting any AI tool to anyone? Weak. Love writers? Specifically recommend AI writing tools to writers. Marketing whiz? Specifically recommend AI-based SEO tools to local businesses. Get the picture?

AI Influencers? Intriguing.

Generic AI avatar? Boring. Stage your AI influencer. AI fashion advice? Snappy. AI art commentary? Cutting edge. Give them a point of view.

E-commerce powered by AI? Smart move.

Use AI to find hot products in a specific market.

Think AI home security. Think anything. Hot products only.

These are just examples. The AI space? It's wide open. Creating boundaries for yourself will stop your growth. Think different.

Want more niche ideas? Of course you do.

My free [newsletter](#)? The kind of AI income secrets most are too scared to use or, honestly, want to keep to themselves. Stuff too hot for a book. Let's leave it at that. Wink, wink.

Bottom line? Your niche is your launchpad. ***Nail it, and you're golden.*** Let's find yours, shall we?

UNDERSTAND YOUR IDEAL NICHE

Let's talk about this. Your business will need a *specific niche* selection to thrive. Picking a niche is dating your business. A perfect dance partner. Someone you vibe with.

The wrong niche? That's two left feet—awkward. Painful.

So, how? Simple. You need ***passion*** and you need ***profit***. Let's break it down.

First—***passion***. What actually gets you going? What would you rather? AI dog groomers? Or AI stock traders? Pick what excites you. Even if it's a little weird. I should add... provided there is a market for it.

Profitability. Passion will drive business success yet we also need profitability to sustain operations.

- ***Demand***—are people searching? ***Ahrefs*** is your friend. So is ***Google Trends***. For example, "AI dog grooming tools" or "best AI dog grooming software."
- ***Competition***. How visible are they online? Three competitors? Good. Three thousand? You're not special anymore.
- ***Pricing***: Can you make money? Look at competitor pricing. Does it match your value?
- And speaking of making a living—***monetization***. What specific methods will you use to generate profit? Affiliate marketing? Selling your own products? Consulting? More is better.

- Finally—*engagement*. To find success you need actual audience interest. Surf through influential figures from your target field to determine the level of engagement their current audience shows. Passionate audiences can be identified through their reactions such as posts getting liked or commented on and being shared.

Select a niche you love that meets all these elements and it will facilitate your path toward victory. No two left feet in sight.

Alright! Going by your AI's assessment your niche appears very appealing. Market size? *Check*. Trends? *Check*. Profitability? Looks good. Next follows the essential phase which is *niche validation*. Data's cool, sure. Validation? That is people, people's complaints, people's wants, reality. Forget guessing games. Let's build niche confidence. *FAST*. Ready?

The popular belief states that if you build something people will naturally flock to it. Yeah, right. This approach only works in movies. Validation is your escape route. Skip it and you face pitfalls.

WHY GUESSING = BUSINESS RUSSIAN ROULETTE

First trap—*confirmation bias*. You see what you want to see. One specific example can be found in *"AI pet portraits."* While AI appears popular with users it shows that many searches target free applications instead of paid services. *Ouch*.

Second trap—*resource drain*. No validation means wasted time and money. Features nobody wants? Bad news. Especially if money is tight.

Third trap—*passion paradox*. You love it. Will they pay? AI offers a cold, hard and helpful stare.

Fourth trap. *Silent assumptions*. You think people get it. Maybe they don't. AI shows knowledge gaps. 'AI' means nothing to some. 'AI saves time' is clear.

Good news—AI helps. It is a detective. It checks your idea three ways—*keywords, rivals, and people*. Less guessing more proof.

1. LET'S LOOK AT KEYWORDS FIRST. AI FINDS NEEDLES IN DATA.

Ahrefs shows search numbers. AI goes deeper. 'AI budgeting' has 50,000 searches. Big deal? What does it mean?

Potential buyers want specific retirement tools or are they just seeking free giveaways? AI identifies the intent.

A keyword might be luring in German seniors while attracting millennials somewhere else. AI spots mismatches.

AI finds *long-tail keywords*. These keywords represent precise and limited searches which indicate strong motivational intent. *Fixed income budgeting tools*. Small but strong niche.

Beginner takeaway? Data? Easy. Patterns? Humanly impossible in data mountains. AI? Needle-in-a-haystack ninja. The process of obtaining data requires no AI help. AI serves as a detection tool for elusive patterns which human analysts cannot notice when processing large data collections.

2. COMPETITOR CLUES: FREE LESSONS

Rivals are not enemies. The triumphs and shortcomings of your competitors give you valuable knowledge without cost.

Market gaps? Spot them. All competitors target 'tech bros'? AI asks: Seniors? Anyone helping them? ***Hello, opportunity***. Where are your competitors blind? AI can see.

AI detects business vulnerabilities like 80% of competitors receiving negative assessments about their inadequate support system? You win with good support.

Warning signs? AI sees them. Big players leaving? ***Red alert***. AI warns you—early. Is the ship sinking?

3. AI PERSONAS. AI PREDICTS MINDS. ALMOST.

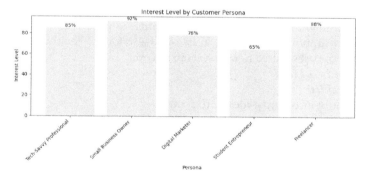

Surveys lie. Friends sugarcoat. Solution? AI personas for interviews. This simulated virtual person features genuine customer requirements and emotional elements.

Concerns? Out in the open. AI persona goes: 'AI and my savings? ***Never!***' Hello, human agent feature. Problem solved. What are their real fears? AI personas spill the tea.

Hidden struggles? No more hiding. Seniors hide tech struggles. AI personas show it. What are they not saying? AI personas do not filter.

Pricing pressure test? Simulated users reject high prices. Senior discount? Yes. $29.99 or no. AI says no. ***Bingo***. Price too high? Too low? AI gives you the sweet spot.

Why this matters? Free audience intel. Deepest fears. Desires. All exposed. AI persona lukewarm? Real audience—colder. AI persona hyped? You're onto something big. In essence, you are getting an AI powered feedback from your focus group for free.

SKIP VALIDATION? HERE'S WHAT YOU'RE RISKING. AND HOW AI CAN HELP. NO VALIDATION MEANS BIG RISKS.

More than just wasting cash. There are other dangers:

- Opportunity cost is real. Wasted months on a dead niche. You could have dominated a good one.
- Competition jungle. Crowded niche? Forget standing out. Fight for scraps. Think rush hour traffic. But for niches.
- Market drowning. Too many clones? Your idea? Swallowed whole. Gone. Too many me-too products? Yours will disappear in the crowd.
- Low Demand: Few paying customers. 'Perfect' niche? Could be nobody's buying. Reality check. Your 'perfect' niche? Might be a ghost town.
- Profit trap. Looks good on paper? Could be broke in months. Don't fall for it.
- Scale? Maybe not. Local niche only? Global dreams die fast.

Avoid this trap. High competition, market saturation, low demand, low profitability, and low scalability. Big problems.

AI saves the day—cheap. AI risk detector for coffee money. Used to cost a fortune. For example, AI might reveal that 62% of users refuse to pay for an "AI travel planner" without human support. *Pivot now*. Years saved—seriously. For the cost of a cup of coffee, AI finds the risks it used to take years to uncover.

Validation Is A Habit.
Not A Checklist.
AI turns doubt into clarity. Ideas into action.

NICHE DOWN?

Now, why is ***niching down*** the move, especially starting out?

AI validates niche ideas. Demand? Market? AI knows. Paradox? *Smaller niche—bigger profit.*

Building a house blind? Madness. Your niche is the exact same way. Everyone yells. Be everything to everyone! ***Wrong.*** Precision? That's freedom. Not limiting. Think *laser*, not *flashlight*. Sharper focus? Way hotter results. Beginner? Seasoned pro? AI-curious rebel? Doesn't matter. Focusing on a specific market segment does not reduce your aspirations but instead removes the confusion. Your audience will become fully engaged at first sight.

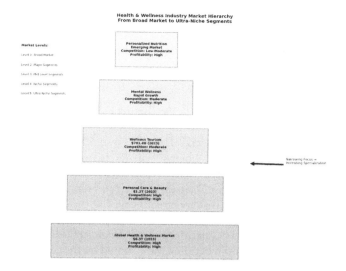

Health & Wellness Industry Market Hierarchy
From Broad Market to Ultra-Niche Segments

WHY 99% OF NICHES DIE (AI DODGES THE BULLETS)

Net too wide or a unicorn chase are the two crash routes. Help everyone on one side. On the other? Help left-handed parrots. With Hand-knit socks. The first is a warzone, the second is a ghost town. Enter AI. Your bias-free detective. It will look at what people search for and what customers desire or wish or how competitors are missing to determine the *Goldilocks zone* where your business should be. Too hot? Too cold? Nah. Just right.

At 68 years old my friend Martha uses online education as her field of interest. AI didn't only provide her with a topic but it created *"bite size history courses for busy professionals"* that received her public attention. The content outline came from a large language model while *Flux* generated the images. No guesswork. Just demand.

YOUR NICHE... YOU NEED TO SHARPEN IT.

Imagine a library that has every single one of the books written 'Non Fiction.' Overwhelming, right? That's broad niches. Sub-niches? Magic's in the specifics. Think pruning a tree. The dead weight cut—strong branches explode.

Think about you. You're hunting. Hunting for a solution. Super specific problem. If you are a senior and you want to do AI for daily finances i.e., just spending tracking and a simple budget. Which grabs you more? Website 1: "Online Business Success for Everyone!" Or? Website 2: "AI Budgeting for Seniors. Control Your Cash!"

Second one wins, right? That's niche power. Speaks directly to you. Instant connection. "Finally, someone gets it!"

The Paradox of Less is More

Beginners freak. Narrow niche? Limits customers? Feels backwards. Wider net should be better. Yeah? Nope. The reality is quite opposite to this especially in the overcrowded online world. Here's why:

- Reduces Competition. Broad niches are battlefields. "Make money online"? You're cannon fodder. You're battling millions. A specific niche? AI-powered content creation? For travel bloggers over 50? It drastically reduces that competition. You become a bigger fish. Yes, it's a smaller pond. Yet, it's more relevant.
- Authority Explodes—Focus? Deep expertise. You become the resource. Go-to guru for that problem. Trust and credibility? Off the charts. Audience flocks to you.
- Marketing? Effective and cheap. Message hits home? Hard. What your customers suffer from and what they want should be the central focus of your messages.
- Conversion Rates? Skyrocket. What was once a casual visitor is now a paying client. Fast. They see you as the answer.
- Premium Pricing. Specialists charge specialist fees. Provided expertise and tailored solutions, people will pay more.

The "Expert" Effect

A general practitioner is valuable, sure. A specialist neurologist? Better. Seen as more expert. Higher fees. The same principle applies to online business.

Niche down? You're the "specialist." Expert vibe? Powerful. Combine with AI? **Unstoppable.**

Niche Statement—3 Questions—Done
This isn't a slogan. It's a filter. Nail these:
- Who's your tribe? "Everyone"? Cop-out. Weak.
- What keeps them up at 2 AM? Real pain points.
- What kind of a unique selling point can you explain when it comes to your offer?

AI's Magic

AI doesn't just brainstorm. It stress-tests. *Google Keyword Planner—SEMrush*—show search heat. AI interprets the data. But it goes **WAY** beyond and can even roleplay as your ideal skeptic. Try this prompt. "Act as a frugal 70-year-old—roast my AI budgeting tool for seniors." Brutal? Maybe. But now you are fixing objections before launching.

A crucial first step is crafting a niche statement, which you will do in the practical exercises. But it's only the beginning. The actual transformative power emerges through living your specific market segment. This means:

- Your content should specifically address the requirements and matters important to your target audience.
- The language should match their preferences.
- AI tools need selection based on their specific problems.
- The development of a niche-based community enabling connections between members.

Your Playbook Move

A niche statement is the first step. The workbook will drill this down. But perfection's the enemy.

Next—AI market research. Know your audience—deeply. Needs—wants—how to serve. Dive deep next. Tomorrow—Niche to Tribe

Bottom line?

AI—not niche pick—flag plant. Let's dig your territory.

KEY TAKEAWAYS

- *Aim small, win big.* Riches are in the niches. *Specificity sells.* Generic AI for everyone? **Fail.** Niche down. *Get paid.*
- Accountants. YouTubers. Writers... *Pick your tribe.*
- Passion and profit? *Your niche soulmates.* Date your business right. Right niche? **Fireworks.** Wrong niche? Two left feet. *Painful.* Love it? Market for it? *Cash in.*
- AI is your detective. It will sniff out winning niches. Keywords, rivals and virtual people are spilling the secrets.
- Validation? Not a checklist, a habit. Skip it? *Business Russian Roulette.* Validation = Coffee Money Risk Detector.
- *Skip Validation, Risk Everything:* Wasted time, lost opportunities, competition hell. AI prevents this. *Cheaply.*
- Small niche, big fish. *Small Niche, Big Bucks.* Paradox? Nope. **Genius.** Dodge the battlefield.
- Niche down, cash up. Dodge the millions. Own your corner.
- Expert effect = *premium pay. Cha-ching!* Specificity = magnetic pull.
- **Niche statement:** It should answer the three questions, *who is your audience, what problem do you solve, and why are you different?*
- Ditch Doubt, Grab Clarity. AI Validation = Action Time. Niche found? Plant your flag. Let's dig.

Niche validated? *Awesome*. We have probed profitable niche identification and validation. Next steps? Practice. Use your workbook. Apply these strategies. Tomorrow? AI for market research. Turn insights into action.

Now, head over to the <u>Workbook Section</u> & complete Day 7 activities.

Day 7: WORKBOOK

THE PASSION-TO-PROFIT MATRIX

You need to *love* what you do in order to perform extraordinary work according to **Steve Jobs**.

Today's activity will take things a step further, and provide you with a powerful framework for finding exactly where your passions intersect with a lucrative opportunity in the *AI* space. This is no ordinary business planning exercise ... it is a systematic way to discover something awesomely valuable: ***business advantage in the marketplace for AI.***

Part 1: Mapping

The first step is building on previous interest exploration.

Review all prior interest inventory exercises you conducted. The upcoming phase will rely on previously developed understanding.

Moving on, we will link your passion areas to certain *AI* capabilities that are revolutionizing those fields of work.

Activity: For each passion, ask *AI* this:

For my passion area in **MY PASSION AREA** please:
   1 Identify. The 5 *AI* technologies currently detonating this industry.
       2 For each technology, provide:
       ° A case study of a business that has already managed to succeed with this technology.
       ° Two untapped opportunities or applications.

○ Explain it like I'm 12
○ Rate difficulty: Low/Medium/High.

Step 3: Building Your Matrix

The fun part now is to establish your own *Passion to Profit Matrix*.

Activity—*Rate & Rank for Riches:*

You can draw out a grid based on rows for your passion areas and then *AI* capabilities as columns.

Each intersection in the matrix requires a rating between 1 and 5 for the following criteria.

Personal Excitement (1=low, 5=high)

Your Knowledge

Market Opportunity (1=saturated, 5=wide open)

Can You Actually Do It?: Easy climb or building Everest?

Your *"power zones"* are the highest combined scores in each cell; add the scores in each cell to identify them.

And hey, guess what? You can use *AI* here as well. Models are now getting decent at math, indeed, who would have thought that? You can then see the current rankings of which current models are best at math here: https://livebench.ai/.

Example:

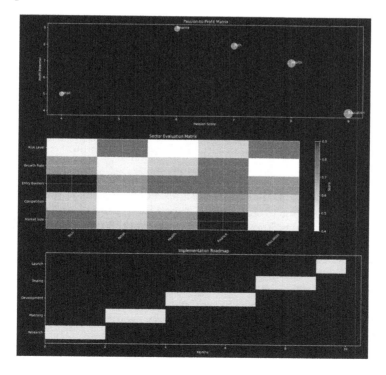

Part 2: Steal These Playbooks

Review how successful *AI* ventures operated so you can create your own *AI* business concept.

Case 1: Maria's Grandma Guardian

Meet Maria. Retired nurse, 40 years in the trenches. Passion? Keeping seniors independent. She had limited technical skills but deep healthcare knowledge.

- Passion Area: Senior healthcare
- AI Capability. Computer vision. Wearable sensors.
- Money Move: Subscription monitoring service

Maria teamed up with a tech co-founder. They then created an *AI* system that could tell with the help of smartphone cameras if there were subtle changes in mobility, medication use and risk of falls. Her secret weapon? Her nursing experience with Parkinson's patients in seniors allowed her to specialize in this area. This made insurance companies very interested in subsidizing her service. Insurance companies now pay her to keep seniors out of hospitals.

Key Success Factors:
• She used her deep healthcare expertise.
• She chose to focus on treating a particular medical issue instead of working with "general health" problems.
• She built partnerships with insurance companies. **Follow the money.**

Case 2: James' Neighborhood Whisperer

James. Real estate agent, 15 years deep. Frustration? Data drowning clients with no clue about the neighborhoods beyond house prices.

- Passion Area. Real estate market analysis.
- AI Capability. Data analytics. Natural Language Generation.
- The business model combines a free *SaaS* tool with premium report offerings.

James built an *AI* brain. James' platform examined local data (of schools, crime, business, social media). It generated neighborhood forecasts in plain English. He mixed public data with his insider knowledge. His secret sauce? Mixing public info with his agent-insider knowledge.

Key Success Factors:
• He spent his time taking a complex data and distilling it into simple insights.
• He targeted a specific pain point (neighborhood selection anxiety)
• He adopted a freemium model to get some credibility before charging.
• The freemium model attracted thousands of agents to join the service.
• Used his 15 years of "gut feeling" as the secret sauce

PART 3. EVALUATION FRAMEWORK.

The Matrix scores are mere starting line. All opportunities in your matrix are not created equal. This framework can be used to evaluate your top candidates.

The *PRIME* Evaluation Framework

Assess these factors from 1-10 for each high-scoring opportunity in your matrix.

- **P - Pain Level:** Are customers' hairs actually on fire?
  - ◦ 1-3: Minor inconvenience
  - ◦ 4-7: Much frustration
  - ◦ 8-10: Proactively looking for a solution to the hair on fire problem they have
- **R. The R factor** examines how easily you can make revenue.
  - ◦ 1-3: Unclear how to monetize
  - ◦ 4-7: A few possible ways to get paid.
  - ◦ 8-10: People are practically begging to pay for this.
- **I - Implementation Speed Run:** MVP in 3 months or 3 years?
  - ◦ 1-3: Over a year—glacial pace.
  - ◦ 4-7: 3-12 months—realistic planning needed.
  - ◦ 8-10: Under 3 months
- **M - Market Readiness.**
  - ◦ 1-3: Education required. Hard sell.
  - ◦ 4-7: Growing awareness
  - ◦ 8-10. Actively seeking.
- **E — Execution Advantage:** You have a unique advantage for this opportunity; what is it?
  - ◦ 1-3: No special advantage
  - ◦ 4-7: Some relevant background or useful connections.
  - ◦ 8-10: Secret weapon level advantage.

Determine the total *PRIME* score (maximum 50 points) for each opportunity. Opportunities with scores above 35 should be taken seriously for further evaluation. The *AI* can be asked to organize and tally these scores for you.

PART 4. CRUSHING YOUR COMPETITION.

Competitive Analysis time.

Having identified some promising opportunities, you now need to determine if the opportunity is crowded.

Activity: For your top 2-3 opportunities, use the following prompts (or adapt them) with your *AI* assistant:

> For the business idea of **[SHORT DESCRIPTION]**, please:
> - Find 3-5 direct competitors (doing almost the same thing).
> - Find 3-5 indirect competitors (solving the same problem differently).
> - Briefly describe for each competitor (direct and indirect):

- ° Their target audience
- ° Their core offering
- ° Their pricing model (if available)
- ° Their apparent strengths and weaknesses.
- • Given the competitive analysis, what are 3 things in particular I can **DO** to make my offering **DIFFERENT** and therefore stand out?
- • Offer 3 examples of a tagline, which would make the uniqueness value of each of the business ideas completely clear to the customer.

Bottom Line:

There is no generic "*AI* for X" idea that your *AI* Business is hiding in. It's that collision between your most frowned upon passion with an unrealized problem. Discover that collision point now, and assign a price.

What distinguishes the winners from the "we help everyone"? They choose *one niched down market segment* before conquering it completely.

Selling yoga mats to "people with legs" is a losing game. Your antidote? Three hyper-targeted exercises. Let's fix that.

ACTIVITY 1: THE NICHE PYRAMID EXERCISE

Objective: Find power by focusing.

Instructions: Use a pen to draw a five-level pyramid for this exercise. Bottom to top: "Broad Market," "Sub-Market," "Niche," "Micro-Niche," and right at the peak, "Ultra-Niche."

The broad market delivers something everybody would purchase.

The Sub-Market category attracts some customer segments yet does not gain universal appeal.

The Niche category serves customers who need this particular item.

Micro-Niche – *"Bingo! These very specific people are desperate for this."*

Ultra-Niche – *"Jackpot! These ridiculously specific people will throw money at this."*

Got it? Good. Pick a **Broad Market**. Something big. *Health & Wellness? Finance? Education? Technology?* The usual suspects.

This AI prompt will assist you in refining each level of your market.

As a market research specialist, help me narrow down the [BROAD MARKET] industry.

For each level give 3 possibilities and brief explanations.

1. Sub-Markets. Within this broad market.

2. Niches within each sub-market

3. Micro-niches. Within each niche.

4. Ultra-niches. Within each micro-niche.

For each level—Broad to Ultra—brainstorm three options. Quick explanations needed. Think:

- • Approximate market size

- Competition level
- Potential profitability
- Digital product opportunities

Complete your pyramid. Choose one option out of each level. Broad Market down to Ultra-Niche. **Boom**—niche path.

Analyze the magic. Notice the change. The target audience gets specific. Their needs get clear. Broad is blurry. Niche is a laser beam.

ACTIVITY 2.

Learn how to make AI write ANYTHING with this *"AI Content Generator" Template.*

Just fill in the blanks:

- Task Prompt: (Create? Explain? Write a poem?)
- Content Type: (Email? Script? Novel?)
- Descriptive: (Funny? Serious? Mysterious?)
- Mood: (Excited? Calm? Philosophical?)
- Goal: (Persuade? Entertain? Convert? Start a cult?)
- Characteristics: (Short? Detailed? Full of dolphin facts?)
- Avoid: (Clichés? Long words?)

Examples:

A Marketer Needs a Newsletter:

"Create a joyful newsletter explaining blockchain to retirees using cat memes. No jargon."

- Task Prompt: Create
- Content Type: Newsletter
- Mood: Joyful
- Goal: Explain
- Characteristics: Cat Memes
- Avoid: Jargon

Designer chasing virality?
- Task Prompt: Design
- Content Type: Instagram post
- Descriptive: Hooking
- Mood: Relaxed
- Goal: Inspire
- Characteristics: Appealing
- Avoid: Too much text

You get the idea!

This template tells AI precisely what you want. And it gets even better...

ACTIVITY 3: THE MAGNETIC NICHE STATEMENT CREATOR
BECAUSE "I HELP PEOPLE" IS A CRIME

Objective: Stop being vague. Get niche. Get rich (maybe).
Instructions: Use the template from Activity 2, or this direct prompt:

> Develop a powerful niche statement for my business which operates within the [YOUR NICHE] market.

> Please follow this formula:
> "[Specific demographic] I help are those that have [specific problem/pain point], and I do this in order to get them to [desired outcome], while [avoiding the common obstacle]."

Let the AI crank out five different niche statement variations using that formula. Five angles, five flavors.

Answer these question to refine your niche statement:

Does it specify enough that someone would realize immediately whether they belong to your target audience?

Is it a painful enough problem that your audience has to solve?

Is there a guarantee of a clear, desirable outcome?

Does it differentiate you from general solutions in the broader market?

Use this AI prompt to try your niche statement:

> Evaluate the effectiveness of this niche statement:
> "[YOUR NICHE STATEMENT]"

> Rate it on:
> 1. Clarity (1-10)
> 2. Specificity (1-10)
> 3. Problem identification (1-10)
> 4. Solution differentiation (1-10)
> 5. Emotional appeal (1-10)

Also, if any of them are less than 8, then suggest improvements in these areas. Finalize your niche statement based on the feedback.

Tomorrow—market research. AI-powered. Go deep on your newly created target audience. Prepare to know them better than they know themselves. Creepy? Effective? You decide.

Ready for the next step? <u>Head to the Day 8 Theory section!</u>

DAY 8: [ENCRYPTED]
AUDIENCE EXTRACTION
AI STALKS. YOU STRIKE. THEY NEVER SEE IT COMING.

P sychology secret that marketers are missing is this: *Demographics are dead.*

Think you know your customer? Think again. The application of AI yesterday helped you define your niche more precisely which proved to be a wise choice. You know what you're selling. Today it is **who** and more importantly, *why they care*. Customer avatars destroy "target audiences" in that regard. Trust me, **customer avatars are key game changer.**

WHY AVATARS BEAT "TARGET AUDIENCES"

Most new entrepreneurs cast a wide net. "Everyone" will love this! Nope. Or they cling to boring age and location data. **Wrong.** Today's digital world is loud. Generic shouts get lost. Imagine yelling "Buy stuff!" in a crowded mall. No thanks. Real connection demands depth. You need to have a sense of their inner world. **Avatars unlock this.**

What is a customer avatar exactly? *Buyer persona*—fancy name. A semi fake but super detailed ideal customer. Not just facts—a story. See them live—in your mind. Walk in their shoes—metaphorically. Real person—not just data. What do they want? What bugs them? What do they actually want? What issues are they dying to resolve?

Let's make this concrete. A grandmother buying AI-generated children's stories isn't just a "female, 60+." She is **Sarah**. Retired teacher. Loves grandkids. She hates too much screen-time for her grandkids. Wants gifts that matter. Or consider a busy parent. They're not just '30 to 45.' They are **drowning**. Work. Family. Chaos. They beg for easy. They crave convenience in every aspect of their life. Likewise, they might feel guilty for not being able to read bedside stories to their children. Generic marketing screams, "Buy this!" The hyper targeted avatars whisper, 'This solves your problem'. When you know Sarah's fears, her dreams, her frantic Google searches at midnight—your message becomes a secret she has to hear.

CRAZY FACT ALERT—name your avatar. Like *"Sarah the Storybook Grandma."* Sales up 68%—yes—sixty-eight percent. **Why?** This is because it activates the brain's social processing centers. And this is what has become known as the *'Sarah Effect'*. Suddenly, you're not just selling an entire crowd, you're focused on letting Sarah know you will solve her very specific problem. Doing this subtle shift does two powerful things. First, it reduces **decision fatigue**. Every marketing choice reduces down: "Would Sarah pay $29.99 for this?" Second, it builds **empathy**. Naturally, you will produce stories that connect with people. Example—"Sarah fears grandkids forget her. Therefore, she sends monthly AI stories with inside jokes." According to research, by the way, even naming your avatar can increase your sales by 68%. That is the *Sarah Effect* and it's **revolutionary.**

Avatars—your secret weapon. Why?

- One—**laser focus marketing**. Know their deepest wants and pains? Your words hit home. Emotionally.
- Two—**product smarts**. Avatars guide product creation. Solve real problems. Give real solutions. No more guessing games. More sales. Higher chance of sales—way higher.
- And third, they lead to **content creation that converts**. Ditch boring stuff. Whenever this content is Avatar focused, it speaks directly to their interests. Their worries. Their dreams. Build trust. Show you're the expert. Drive sales. You know which words to use, which platforms to use, and which offers will be irresistible.

Demographics are very shallow: age, gender, zip code. But **psychographics?** *That's where the magic happens.* Think deeper—**values.** What's actually important to them? **Interests**—hobbies, passions? How do they spend time, cash, **Lifestyle. Attitudes**: Their opinions and beliefs? **Motivations**—what pushes them to act? What are the **pain points** for them like 'what keeps them up at night?' What do they desperately want to solve? Marketing and products become irresistible. Grandma Sarah buying AI stories? It's not just an AI generated children's book they are buying. They are buying a **legacy**. A way to **bond**.

AI FUNCTIONS AS AN EXPERT AVATAR CREATOR AND DESIGNER.

It was traditionally a really intensive process to create customer avatars. Research. Surveys. Talk to people. Still good—but slow. **AI is the shortcut. AI tools are data ninjas**. Forums. Reviews. Find common threads. Interests they share. AI reads searches. Support tickets. Online talk. Uncovers hidden problems. Even avatar profiles can be made with AI. Names. Stories. Pictures. AI digs deep. Faster than any human group. It sees language. Trends. Even emotions in customer words.

But—AI is a start. A tool. **You are still THE avatar architect.** Refine AI ideas. Add your smarts. Ensure that your avatar is actually genuine. Captures the true customer. **Avatars aren't just fun. They are strategy. Serious business.**

So, quick recap. Yesterday? You found what, now who, you are selling. **Ditch basic demographics. Dive into psychographics. Make detailed avatars. Use AI to help. Connect with people deeply.** Then—you don't just sell. You solve problems. Build trust. Give real value.

Alright. *Facts time?*

90% of the world's data? ***Boom***—created in just the last two years. Sounds wild, right? The kicker, however, is that *73 percent of market researchers are drowning.* Insights can't be processed fast enough to be able to do anything. Sound familiar? You are not drowning in data. **The right tools** are what you thirst for.

Most people see more data as the answer. **Nope.** That's the myth. This is not *data overload*, it's *gold mine for strategy.* Winners in the *AI* age? They don't hoard tools. They use them like scalpels.

Traditional market research? *Searching for the needle in a haystack* seems like the description here. *AI* totally flips that script. Now it's not you that is hunting, it's the magnet that's pulling that needle right to you.

But there's a catch. The tools are not created equal. How to discover them and evaluate them? That's what distinguishes wasting time from unlocking breakthroughs. Some are versatile *Swiss Army knives.* Others? Scalpels. Your mission? Discover the ones that make your flaws into *fatal advantages.*

Free tools? Free like a puppy on a parking lot. Cute—but comes with costs. Think about it, you build your competitor intel using a so called free tool. Great. You later discover that it is also selling your insights. **Worse?** You train their *AI.* Your ***COMPETITOR's***. For free. Ouch.

PLAYING THE LONG GAME

AI tools are powerful, and indeed mirrors of what you are willing to pay for. Data sharing is how free tools usually monetizes. Before diving in, ask:

> • "Am I training my competitors through the use of my niche's sensitive data to train their models?"
> • "Which jurisdictions host their servers?"
> • "Is there anything in this tool's TOS which allows them to resell my industry insights."

And hey. Real talk. Do you even care the slightest about privacy? Be honest with yourself.

This isn't paranoia. **It's prudence.** Sustainable advantage requires ethical infrastructure.

AI AS YOUR TOOL-WHISPERER

The unfair advantage beginners have here is using *AI* to evaluate other *AI* tools. For instance:

> • "What are the best 3 free competitive analysis tools for Amazon KDP and what are their limitations for a solo entrepreneur?"

> • "Compare Tool A and Tool B for [whatever task]. First of all, focus on how easy they are to use right away, and if I can actually get my data out later."

> • "I need a list of tools in [your industry] where you can access the API and easily integrate with Zapier."

Give your *AI* text generator a tool's *FAQ* page with the instruction 'summarize the onboarding process to a non-tech person in 3 steps'

Actually, you can create your own evaluation framework.

Command your *AI*:

> "Create a scoring system for CRM tools. A couple requirements: Offline data syncing, cost shall not exceed $50 a month, and it will work with Slack. Weight those priorities accordingly."

Pro tip. Ask *AI* to analyze *Product Hunt* comments or comments on *GitHub*. An example is:

> "Summarize any complaints against [Tool X] and [Tool X]'s mobile app from the past 6 months."

HEAR YOUR CUSTOMERS—FOR FREE.

Here's a thought experiment. Imagine a room. And it is jam packed with your *ideal* customers. Secrets are shouted—with deep desires and real pain. Only you understand the language. **AI is your translator.** Picture *Sherlock Holmes* in level of insight, *Watson* in the work ethic, minus the Victorian age budget.

Stop Guessing. Start Detective-ing.

People are complex. Their wants are hidden. Hard to say out loud. Amazon reviews? *Treasure troves.* A single complaint that a children's book was 'too short'? Not just a whine. *It's a shout.* A parent wants to enjoy calm in the midst of chaos. **AI gets it.** It can read feelings under words. Not just counting complaints. *It's Sherlock with software.*

The Psychology of Pain Points

People buy fixes. Not just stuff. A bad toy? It's not about toys. A parent feels lost. **Validation as a caregiver** is what they are looking for. AI sees this. It analyse language in reviews, social media. *"Am I failing as a parent?"* AI finds these hidden cries. Then you know what to do.

Demographics Lie. *Emotions* Don't.

Age/income data? Basic. **Emotional intel?** *Goldmine.*

Customer raves *"This storybook made my kid's eye's light up—finally, not more junk"*. They're actually confessing:

- Guilt about clutter
- Craving meaningful moments
- Pride in nurturing their child's imagination.

The number of reviews and posts available exceeds what any person can safely handle. To the extent that AI can filter the data vastness into easily accessible information, it is a filter.

Your Silent Business Partner.

AI is not a robot. It's like a people expert. You prompt it to roleplay your customer avatar. It is similar to talking to their mind. Describe the customer as a teacher who wants a side job. AI feels their feelings.

Training AI to be your stressed single parent, retiree dealing with tech for the first time gives you direct, unfiltered visceral feedback.

The trick? Feed it details. Use *'Sarah: 34, hides in the bathroom to eat Hershey's, thinks her kids think she is mediocre'* instead of 'busy mom.' Raw confessions suddenly spew back: *"I'm too tired to be Pinterest perfect, but I can't fail them."* These emotional confessions? *They're gateways.* They show you precisely what to say in your marketing. The fears to calm. The desires to amplify.

Cut through the noise. AI gives you clarity.

The most common mistake that the beginners make is getting lost in the data. AI makes the data firehose into a stream. 100 reviews include:

- 32 ""too pricey"" comments (translation: *"prove to me why it's worth it"*).
- 19 "easy to tweak" praises (screaming: ***"Lead with this!"***).
- 7 complaints about "shipping delays" – A logistical worry to address preemptively.

This isn't just research. **It's strategic foresight.** To teach the AI to sort data, prioritize it and reframe it, you are not simply solving today's problems. You are anticipating the trend of tomorrow. Without looking creepy, you really are reading your customer's minds. And definitely without spending a fortune.

What's next? You will spot missed opportunities from competitors with your *AI* assistant at hand. The time has come to identify their weaknesses.

. . .

The famous ancient Chinese military strategist **Sun Tzu** said,

> '*If you know yourself & know your enemy, you need not fear the result of a hundred battles.*'

This of course doesn't mean we're talking actual battles, but the rule nevertheless applies in a business world. It's vital to understand your competition to have a better position for success.

You know your customer. Good. You used AI tools. Smart. Research on the cheap —Indiana Jones on a budget. Excellent. Good start for your AI business. Now—look outward. Your competitors aren't enemies.

Forget stealing ideas. Let's talk about winning. Not by copying. Advantage time. Advantage in business is about observing, learning, and innovating. Knowing their plans. Finding secret openings. All ethical. All AI.

COMPETITIVE INTELLIGENCE.

Secret weapon? Their Content is a Brain Scan.

Seriously. Not only is competitors' content marketing, it's also a psychological blueprint. Their website's a confession letter. Their website copy whispers about their customers' deepest desires. Their tweets? Therapy sessions With AI. Without the filter.

Three Layers of AI Brain Scans

What Are They Really Selling?

A competitor's text is totally strategic. That "*About Us*" page? It is a deliberately crafted identity manifesto. AI? It's your linguistic Sherlock Holmes. It uncovers:

- Audience fingerprints: Subconscious clues—who they really target—age— fears—dreams they sell back to them.
- Emotional Triggers. Selling safety? Status? Simple life?

It is looking for weaknesses such as: Overused phrases, vague promises, missed opportunities.

For instance, when rivals are seen yelling "*Get rich quick*", AI senses (and suppresses) the collective eye roll. Position yours as "*Get rich while sleeping.*"

Social Media—Truth Serum

Instagram and Facebook are business reality shows... Websites are polished lies. Social media is raw. Unfiltered. Reality. AI sees past likes.

- Content Cadence. Daily posts? That might signal desperation. Weekly— confident?

- Tone Shifts. LinkedIn—stiff. TikTok—silly. Identity crisis?
- Lots of posts. Few comments. Shouting into the void?

Pro Insight. The focus of engagement should be to create strong ties not increase popularity. AI can spot emotional hooks. Fear of missing out? Hunger for community? AI knows. Optimizes for your niche.

Visuals—Subconscious Sell.

Brains accept images 60,000x faster than the words. Competitor visuals are psychological warfare. Multimodal AI to the rescue.

- Color psychology. Blue = trust (finance). Red = urgency (limited offers).
- Composition secrets. Over cluttered layout speaks 'there are too many things' and simple layout says 'we have this under control'.
- Pattern recognition. Visual motifs displayed in patterns help customers recognize the brand through constant exposure.

Golden Rule. Be the peacock in a flock of pigeons. Your aim should not be to duplicate designs but to make your work different from what others have done. The use of AI to produce personalized visuals becomes a competitive edge when every market participant chooses stock imagery.

Competitive intelligence is about understanding those underlying principles in the business world. What are the ingredients of other businesses' success? Analyze these key areas:

- ***Value Proposition.*** What unique value do they offer the customers? How do they position? This is not limited to their features of the product or service, it's the full experience, along with what benefits they provide. Audience tells: Same crowd as you? Good. Find their ignored 10%.
- ***Marketing and Sales.*** How do they attract and convert the customers? What social media, email, paid advertising do they use, etc. What words communicate their offers and how do they present themselves to customers? Evaluating their marketing practices will show which industry approaches succeed while others fail.
- ***Pricing and Positioning.*** What are they pricing their products? Budget-friendly bargain? Something in the lucrative middle? Premium brand aura? Budget brand blitz? It helps you to determine your pricing.
- ***Strengths & Weaknesses:*** SWOT time. Rivals' good—bad points. Find where you beat them. Hit their weak spots.

Remember, **Sun Tzu** said it best: "*If you know the enemy & know yourself, you need not fear the result of a hundred battles.*" But what you have now is AI as your partner.

. . .

Let's talk about planning. But **not overplanning**. You require a business plan no matter how you feel about them. Or do you? The best plan is no plan—except when it is. Confused? Good. Let's talk **smart planning**. You should always choose action over planning. *Always*. Err on the side of doing. In fact, it's really easy to hide procrastination in the guise of planning, but you still need what I call **flexible planning**.

Ever played chess? The grandmasters aren't reacting to the board but are ten moves ahead with their thoughts. Your business? **Chess game**. Life? **Chess meets poker**. Plan. But be ready to play the hand.

Why Blueprints?
Simple. They're *Not Dinosaurs Yet*.

There is more need for blueprints than ever. Research on the market is not just the data, it's the crucial intelligence gathered. Beginners get bogged down. With spreadsheets. Seasoned entrepreneurs focus on the **key 20% of information** that drives **80% of the results**. **AI is your intel curator**. It cuts the noise. Finds patterns humans miss.

The shocker here is that planning is needed now more than ever. But **old plans? *Dead*. 50-page plans? *Dinosaurs*.** This is the fast digital world. **Adapt or die.**

Strategic choices. Less is truly more. AI makes smart to-do lists. It finds high-impact, low-effort tasks first. Not just lists. It cross-references audience pain. Competitor weakness. It finds the fast wins. Think **GPS**. Traffic jam ahead? AI reroutes you. No more crowded markets. AI finds open roads.

Today's successful online businesses are built upon **three fundamental planning pillars** which, with the aid of AI capabilities, have all radically shifted.

1. Pillar One—Audience. Always Audience.

Traditional planning starts with what you want to offer. **Who you're serving** is the starting point of **strategic planning**. Every seriously profitable online business I've studied? They all obsess over **audience desires, frustrations, and behaviors**. Then they create solutions.

2. Message-Market Alignment

Alex Hormozi has this down, this is about creating such offers that people feel dumb if they said no. His book, *"$100M Offers"*? The bible of offer creation. Simple framework. Anyone can use it.
Hormozi's value equation? Genius.
Hormozi breaks down offer creation into a value equation:

- **Dream Outcome.** What is the dream outcome for your audience (the ultimate win). Nail that down.
- **Reduce Perceived Risk:** Lower their fear of failure or wasted time.

- **Minimize the level of operational effort required:** Make the way to success appear doable and easy.
- **Shorten Perceived Time to Results:** Have them get wins soon, not in two years.
- **Stack value so high—price looks tiny.** Value MUST outweigh cost—by miles.

Offer immense value at a low price. Seriously. Offer someone a $100 bill for $20. Deal? Every. Single. Time. A **killer offer** is THAT powerful.

The principle is clear for anyone, beginner or expert. Don't merely sell a product. Package a solution. Remove objections preemptively. You do need to deliver results customers truly value. Hormozi's book is **required reading** for creating high-converting offers. Trust me on this.

3. Pillar Three—Distribution Domination. Find Your People.

What methods do you use to locate your customers? Simple. Get your amazing offer in front of the right eyes. *$100m Leads* by Alex Hormozi is another goldmine.

It is simple to the core but powerful. Stop chasing everyone. Focus. Be precisely where your ideal customers already gather. What Hormozi teaches is that lead gen isn't fancy tactics. Knowing where your prospects "drink". **Watering holes**. Position yourself there. Right message. Right place. Right time.

Leveraging AI—Keep Your Edge.

Business planning has been democratized with AI, but the technology is not the advantage. **How you use it is**. Every entrepreneur has access to similar tools. Few use them for strategic thinking.

What I see in top online business owners? They do not simply query AI for answers. They **collaborate with it**. They **think with AI**. They add insights, experiences, intuition. AI expands. Validates. Challenges.

This **human-AI collaboration** creates business plans that are not only technically sound. They are also uniquely authentic. AI handles data crunching. Pattern recognition. Humans add the heart. Empathy. Creativity. Purpose. That's connection.

Next: your executive summary. A snapshot of your vision. In seconds, not hours.

B attlefield mapped. Now the AI Business Blueprint Workshop. Insights to action. Knowledge without action? Just trivia. **WE BUILD EMPIRES HERE.** Let's go.

KEY TAKEAWAYS

- *Demographics are dead. Long live avatars!* Stop selling to "everyone." Know Sarah, her fears, her midnight Google searches. Solve her specific problems.
- **AI creates avatars fast.** But you are the architect. Add heart. Build trust.
- Forget "buy stuff". Quality marketing lets customers feel understood by sharing their challenges.
- Your AI system has the capability to understand your customers' feelings as well as analyze data. Let it feel their feels.
- ***Competitor Content: A Free Brain Scan (Ethically!).*** Seriously. Websites, social media, all reveal their customers' desires. Their website is a confession. AI reads between the lines. AI reveals their secrets. Find their weaknesses. Win.
- Data is everywhere. Researchers drown. **AI is the life raft.** Use it wisely.
- Free AI tools? Cute, but risky. ***DO NOT TR AI N YOUR COMPETITORS FOR FREE.*** Read the fine print.
- **AI Sherlock is Open for Business.** Stop guessing customer needs. The data deluge has hidden desires, and AI finds them. Deduction, not data overload.
- ***Human + AI = Empire Builder.*** AI crunches data. You offer your intelligence and charisma as well as your enthusiasm. Team up and conquer.
- RIP 50-page plans. ***Agile Blueprints are King.*** Think chess, not checkers. AI is your strategic coach. Calculator. Faster and deeper than any human. Plan smart, act fast.
- **Emotions sell.** Demographics tell lies. AI reads people's emotions in reviews and social media. *Goldmine alert!*
- ***Audience First, Always. Solve Their Problems.*** Stop pushing random products. Obsess over what your audience wants and is in pain with. Remove all objections before they arise. Make the value so high, the price seems trivial. Solve their problems, and the sales will follow.
- **Distribution Domination:** Find Your Customer Watering Hole. Focus where they already gather.
- **Action over perfection**, do not use planning to procrastinate, just start.

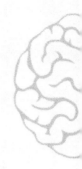

DAY 8: WORKBOOK

Ditch Days of Work. AI Does Research in Minutes.
"90% of Market Research Time—GONE. Thanks to AI."
There's no oxygen to your business without market research. Google search combined with basic chatbots provide the current means of operation. Coming to a sword duel with a butter knife is how it feels. Either you end up with outdated intel or confident-sounding nonsense (*"Hallucinations,"* as we call them. No, this is not of the psychedelic kind).

Tools Matter.

Online business is a knife fight. Dull tools? You bleed out. Market research used to be slow torture. Now? The introduction of AI research tools creates fundamental transformation in the market. Think faster success. Think more money. This isn't a tweak. *It's a total flip*. AI assistants now have both intellectual abilities and access to the internet. Online entrepreneurs—*wake up*.

CHATBOTS ARE DUMB. MEET SMART RESEARCH AI.

You've used basic chatbots. They are OK for simple questions. However, they do not perform well in deep market research. Their data is old. They tend to hallucinate – that is, make things up.

Which is why platforms like *Monica, Merlin, Ninjachat* and *Perplexity* emerge. Fundamentally different. Consider them as the deep research assistants. You do not have to rely on pre trained knowledge. These tools can do the following.

- **Access the Live Web:** They have built-in internet access, allowing them to pull information from the most up-to-date sources.

- They don't just link. ***They dig.*** Scrape. Hundreds of pages. Articles. Data. Everything.
- **They analyze.** Find trends. Compare facts. Make sense of it all.
- **Cite Their Sources:** They show their work. You can check the data sources and investigate further.

Result? Days of work—gone. Weeks—poof. Now it's minutes. Seriously. This all is done citing sources. You get real analysis. **Boom.**

One Tool to Rule Them All.

And here's the kicker: *Monica* and *NinjaChat* provide access to *Perplexity*. There's no need to pay for multiple individual AI tools. One stop AI shop. Pictures a single tool that can:

- Conduct comprehensive market research (as we just described).
- Research trends related to retirement planning during the early morning hours of 8 AM
- Code your sales page by 9
- Create social media visuals by 9:30
- Write email copy by 10

A single workspace gives you complete AI-powered assistance for all your requirements without requiring you to move between platform subscriptions.

THE AI RESEARCH ASSISTANT CHALLENGE

See for Yourself

This challenge shows you the gap. Dumb chatbot vs. smart AI.

Activity Overview

In this hands – on challenge, you will use AI research assistants to address real business problems from basic to advanced approaches.

What You'll Need

- Access to a basic AI chatbot (ChatGPT free version works)
- Access to an AI research assistant (*Monica AI* is highly recommended, as it provides access to *Perplexity's* powerful research capabilities within a comprehensive platform. You can also try *Perplexity* separately.)
- Timer. Because time is money.

The Challenge Structure

10 minutes: Part 1: The Basic vs. Advanced Experience

For this, use a basic AI chatbot.
Ask both tools:

"What are the most profitable digital niches for beginners in 2025? List top options with their profit potential and difficulty levels.

Advanced Research Assistant: Using *Monica* (or *Perplexity*), ask the exact same question.

Now, compare. What do you see?

- **Up-to-Date Info?** Which tool holds data that is the most current?
- **Real Market Data?** Stats and figures? Who's got 'em?
- **Citations?** Sources you can check? **Mandatory.**
- **Actionable Stuff?** Info you can use right now?

Part 2: The Time-Saving Challenge (15 minutes)

Pick a Niche. "Retirement guides." "AI prompts." "Senior fitness." You choose.

Traditional Research (7 minutes): Use Google search and manually visit websites to answer:

- Market size for this niche
- Top 3 competitors
- Average price points
- Key customer pain points

Advanced Research Assistant (3 minutes): Use *Monica* (or *Perplexity*) with this prompt:

Give a complete market analysis for the [YOUR NICHE] digital product niche, including:
- Current market size. Plus growth projections.
- Unique Selling Points of top 3 competitors.
- The average price points and pricing strategies.
- The main problems and needs which customers experience.
- The most effective marketing channels for the niche are.
Specify your data and cite the sources.

Compare Times. Do the Math. **How much time did you save?** Think about implementing this solution for every piece of research. Tasks that would have used to take 10-20 hours? Now under an hour. That's over 90% time saved. **Boom.**

Amazon-level businesses use similar AI tools to cut research time from weeks to hours and get better results.

As a solo entrepreneur, you now have access to the same power.

Part 3: Challenge: The 'Aha Moment' (20 minutes)

Now, let's imagine you have a complex task to perform – creation of your first passive income product.
Use *Monica* (or *Perplexity*) or Choose Your Assistant.
Initial Prompt:

> What I want to do is make a profitable digital product in the [YOUR NICHE] space. Please help me with:
> • Give ideas for 5 products with the profit estimates.
> • Provide the estimated time to create it, required skills/tools and approximation of selling price for each idea.
> • Analyze competition level for each idea (low, medium, high)
> • Recommend the best option for a beginner to start with and explain why
> • Outline the exact next steps I should take to create this product
> Add relevant market data with your sources cited.

Review and Note:

- Was it comprehensive?
- Includes any action steps?
- How long would this have taken manually?

Follow-Up Prompt:

> Please help me with the 'SELECTED PRODUCT IDEA'
> 1 Develop an extensive outline containing between five and seven main sections.
> 2 Suggest key points for each section.
> 3 I need to identify the specialized knowledge I will need to continue research.
> 4 Provide three distinct features that could differentiate this product from its market competitors.
> 5 Recommend tools to help create this product efficiently

Comparing Your Experience
Reflect on the differences:
• **Basic Chatbots:**

- Provide general information based on training data
- These are often without particular sources or citations.
- No current market view—living in the past.

• **Advanced Research Assistants:**

- See real time information regarding anything from across the web.
- Cite their sources like a PhD student on Red Bull
- Can be used to handle complex, multi part business questions.
- Save a lot of time compared to manual research

AI research is used even by giants to stay ahead. For you as a solo entrepreneur? These tools are the levelers. They allow you to create a successful business online. **Essential to win.** *Not nice to haves anymore.*

Your move. Tools are ready. Time's ticking. And that niche isn't going to research itself.

CUSTOMER AVATAR BOOTCAMP

Want a ***300% Boost in Sales?*** Want customers who *get* you? This challenge is your answer.

Activity Overview

This challenge unfolds in five stages. Each one builds on the last. The end result? A customer avatar so detailed, it will tell you what to do.

Stage 1

The objective here is to convert cold demographics into a named persona with basic characteristics.

Steps:

- List the usual suspects: age range, location, income, education of your target customer.
- Pick a name that *screams* your target (No "Customer McCustomerface")
- This AI prompt will help you write a basic background story.

> Create a short background story for a customer avatar [NAME] is [AGE] years old, lives at [LOCATION] and makes [INCOME LEVEL], also [NAME] has [EDUCATION LEVEL]. Include their occupation, current living situation, and include one daily challenge they face with regards to [YOUR PRODUCT/SERVICE CATEGORY]. Always try to maintain a genuine human tone.

Stage 2

Psychographics

Now we must discover your avatar's true goals, values, fears and hopes.

Steps:

This AI prompt helps you discover psychographic information.

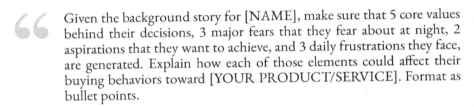

> Given the background story for [NAME], make sure that 5 core values behind their decisions, 3 major fears that they fear about at night, 2 aspirations that they want to achieve, and 3 daily frustrations they face, are generated. Explain how each of those elements could affect their buying behaviors toward [YOUR PRODUCT/SERVICE]. Format as bullet points.

Read what the AI spits out. Does it feel right? Trust your gut. Trash the BS. Add your own genius.

Stage 3

What we can do in Stage 3 is to perform the ***Immersion Experience*** - Walk in Their Digital Shoes.

The mission is to understand which virtual locations an avatar uses while browsing the online world. What types of cat videos interest their online persona? (Okay maybe not cat videos).

Steps:

This prompt will help generate a list of your avatar's online behaviours.

> For my customer avatar [NAME] with the following profile [INSERT YOUR PSYCHOGRAPHIC PROFILE FROM STAGE 2], generate:
>
> 1 Web sites they probably frequent on a daily or at least regular basis.
>
> 2 The three social media platforms they prefer; and, how each one is used.
>
> 3 Even down to 3, 4 types of content they engage with the most (in videos, articles, podcasts, etc.)
>
> 4 The four types of influencers or thought leaders who interest them.
>
> 5 The hours during the day they are most active online
>
> Format as a "Digital Day in the Life" timeline.

Test this profile by spending 15 minutes browsing as your avatar would. Check out one of the recommended websites to determine if the content matches your avatar's psychographic characteristics.

Stage 4

Stage 4 consists of finding the ***visual manifestation*** for your avatar.

Give it a face. Because faces are memorable. Words? Not so much.

Steps:

Use an all in one tool like Monica or any AI text to image tool with this prompt to generate an image of your avatar:

> Create a realistic portrait photograph of [NAME], a [AGE] year old [GENDER] who works as a [OCCUPATION]. They are both [KEY PERSONALITY TRAIT] and [SECOND KEY PERSONALITY

TRAIT]. As for the image, they should be in their [LOCA-TION/SETTING related to your business] and display a [EMO-TIONAL STATE] face. Do not show any text in the image.

Save this image and refer to it when making business decisions. Tape this portrait to your monitor. The visual reminder helps maintain customer-centricity.

Stage 5: Decision Matrix – Avatar Action Plan

The objective is to create a decision making tool through your avatar to direct business choices.

Steps:

This AI prompt builds your cheat sheet. Use it wisely.

> Create a decision matrix for evaluating business opportunities based on my customer avatar [NAME]. Include:
> 1 5 key questions I should ask about any marketing message before sending it to [NAME]
> 2 The 3 product features that would have [NAME] noticing them right away
> 3 2 potential objections [NAME] might have about my offerings
> 4 A 10 point scoring system on how well a new business idea fits [NAME]'s needs
> Format this as a printable worksheet with clear sections.

Use your matrix. Rate your business. Are you serving your avatar? Or are you just guessing?

Measuring the "Sarah Effect"

Note down the current business metrics (conversion rates, engagement rates, customer satisfaction)

Use your new avatar insights on one marketing campaign or product.

After implementation, measure the same metrics and calculate the percentage increase

That's your "Sarah Effect."

STAGE 6:

Time for an "interview." Our niche for example purposes is AI Powered Fitness coaching for seniors. The goal is to ask questions that will reveal even more about their motivations, pain points, and desires related to fitness and using technology for coaching.

Text Prompt to Initiate the Avatar Interview with your AI Tool:

> You will now play the part of 'Arthur, the Active Ageless' who happens to be a 72 years old retired accountant as the perfect customer for an AI powered fitness coaching SaaS for seniors. Arthur values his independence and health. He is somewhat tech-hesitant but open to simple solutions. Keeping active and healthy without either injury or feeling

completely swamped is his 'Daydream Dilemma'. Answer the following questions as if you are Arthur, speaking in the first person. Give detailed and thoughtful responses showing Arthur's personality and motivations as we have defined them.

Example Interview Questions for Arthur, the Active Ageless:

- Arthur, what bothers you about fitness?
- What's your #1 health goal?
- Does it sound robot nonsense when I mention an 'AI fitness coach'?
- What elements would convince you to invest money in this service?

After the Interview Reflection:
Read Arthur's answers. Anything surprise you? New pain points? New desires? Did Arthur just rewrite your business plan in his answers? Probably.
How does this refine your understanding of your real senior customers?

Final Challenge: The Avatar Expansion
If you have more than one customer type... No problem.
Use this prompt to build your avatar family. However, not too many – families are complicated.

> Based on my primary customer avatar [NAME] and my business [YOUR BUSINESS], suggest 2 additional complementary customer avatars that I might target. For each, provide:
> 1 A name. Brief demographics.
> 2 How they differ from my primary avatar
> 3 Which particular products or services would be most appealing to them?
> 4 For each, how I might have to change my messaging.

This *Avatar Evolution Challenge* is your shortcut to customer understanding. Forget guessing. *Know* your customer. It is how entrepreneurs increase conversions massively. For those who use detailed avatars, conversion increases up to *300%*. That's not a typo.

Successful entrepreneurs do not sell to faceless demographics, but move to solve problems for people that they truly understand. This challenge helps you do exactly that.

ACTIVITY: *THE COMPETITOR BRAIN SCAN & ADVANTAGE FINDER*

This activity is designed to help you put the theory of *AI-driven competitor intelligence* into immediate action.

Why This Matters

Most business owners look at competitors superficially. Most people check competitor prices. Maybe a quick website peek. *Amateur hour stuff.* However, you are not like them, are you? So with your AI on your side, you're able to find insights that they are completely blind to. Ninety-nine percent of businesses are missing this. **Seriously.**

The AI Competitor Detective Challenge

Step 1: Name Your Nemeses

First up, list 3-5 competitors. Not sure who they are? Throw this prompt at your AI:

> In my launch of [your business], I'm going after [your audience]. Who's already winning here? Provide me with the business names along with their URLs and a clear explanation of their success strategy.
>> After getting your list, choose *one aspect* to analyze:
>> • Their product/service features
>> • Their pricing strategy
>> • How they flirt with customers
>> • Their marketing Jedi mind tricks
>> • Their USP

Step 2: AI Data Collection

Forget endless manual research. We're automating this.

Quick-Start Setup:

Fire up **Google Alerts**. **Free**. Set one up for each competitor's brand name. **Done.**

Website Autopsy Prompt

Copy. Paste. Profit. Use this prompt for some initial intel:

> Analyze the website copy of [Competitor Website URL]. Sniff out their social media. Give me:
>> 1 Their main products/services and pricing
>> 2 Are they formal, informal, humorous, serious, etc.?
>> 3 Recent launches
>> 4 The primary pain points they claim to solve for customers
>> 5 What seems to be their unique selling proposition
>> 6 Who is their ideal target audience based on their language?

Step 3: Crack Their Code

Here's where it gets juicy. *This is where most businesses stop.*

Review Decoder

The review analysis and comparison to the value proposition is a powerful way to find the gaps.

> Use these customer reviews and social media comments from customers of [Competitor Name]. Based on these reviews, answer the following:
> What are customers' unmet needs, top 3 frustrations? *Exact customer language—word for word—important.* Any new trends in customer wants they miss? Summarize the main reasons customers are happy with this product.

Image Analysis Prompt:
Use a multimodal AI model for this one.

> **Target: Enemy Website Decryption**
> I will just share the screenshots of the competitor's product page and social media post.
> Explain how the rivals build their brand identity through visual elements.
> 1 What feelings are they attempting to generate
> 2 How do the images display their products to customers? Is it cluttered, clean, modern, traditional, etc.?
> 3 When trying to reach the [target audience], what visual elements are definitely missing?
> 4 Generate a word cloud of the most noticeable visual elements & themes in this image.
> 5 Can my business establish a unique appearance on the market without losing our target audience?

Market Gap Analysis Prompt:

> Using all available information about [Competitor Name] help me detect possible market opportunities.
> 1 Which customer groups do they currently neglect?
> 2 Which price ranges does their business fail to address?
> 3 What would be the other services that if offered could complement their core offering?
> 4 Do customers have unmet emotional requirements?

Step 4: Insight Generation
Found a gap? Time to own it. Use this prompt:

> Based on my competitor intel [paste findings], show me:
> 1 Biggest underserved opportunity.

2 3 ways my business could uniquely address this gap

3 How I could position my offering to emphasize this difference

4 What resources I would need to execute on this opportunity

Step 5: Action Planning

Insights need action. 30-day plan time. Strategic prompt:

> Help me create a 30-day action plan to take advantage of this competitive opportunity: [paste your chosen opportunity].
> The plan should include:
> 1 3 quick wins I can start immediately
> 2 To show my unique approach, a content strategy
> 3 How to test my positioning with minimal cost
> 4 The metrics I will track to know if my approach is working

The Path to Becoming the Customer: *The Secret Power Move*

Go deeper than most competitor analysis ever goes. This prompt gives you extraordinary insight.

> What I would like to get is a grasp of the entire customer journey of a person who uses [Competitor's] service.
> Be a potential customer and take me through:
> 1 The complete purchasing journey from beginning to end.
> 2 The highs and lows throughout in terms of emotions
> 3 The critical times when trust is created or destroyed.
> 4 Hidden customer fears.
> 5 The specific moment when a customer would consider switching to an alternative

Seriously, this one exercise can reveal more than weeks of traditional research.

We will expand these insights into a complete AI-enhanced business plan during our work tomorrow. Your identified competitive gaps today will feed straight into the positioning strategy.

If your competitor's reading this let's hope they skimmed.

R eady for the next step?
      Head to the Day 9 Theory section!

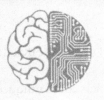

Day 9: EXECUTE.
From Vision to Action

Alright. You have immersed yourself in data and now can describe your audience more accurately than they understand themselves. Good. It's time to transition from information collection to implementation.

Forget old business plan templates. We're leveling up with AI.

Business plans, right? *A bad first date experience indeed.* Bad first dates in paper form. Forced. Awkward. Moving through the process without enthusiasm you think about how long this will drag out. But hold up. This is different. This entire process is about to receive **AI-enhancements**. More fun!

The Real Reason Why You Are Actually Avoiding Business Planning. And It's Not What You Think.

Fear is the reason why people avoid plans. Not laziness. Fear of wrong paths. Fear of wasting time on paperwork. Staring at financials that say *"You'll die in 6 months"*? Yep.

Beginners and career-switchers suffer most. *"Bad math?" "Delusional ideas?"* Relax. This is precisely where **AI transforms the game.** Here's how:

- No blank page paralysis + with drafts you can actually use
- Instant *"Is this garbage?"* feedback—no weeks of waiting. Boom.
- A simulator runs parallel universes to offer you worst-case scenario outcomes

What Makes an *AI-Enhanced* Business Plan Actually Valuable?

- Value proposition that has been refined by AI such that it is **laser focused**.
- Market segments found through AI research are **clearly identified**.
- Weaknesses told as they are through **SWOT analysis**

- Financials that can bend when reality shifts, which for obvious reasons, it always does.
- Deadlines that make you **productively busy**, not guilty.

Notice what's missing? The endless market reports you could Google in five seconds, the boring and unfocused introductions. Generic stats (rivals copy-paste already). **Waste of time. Good riddance. Skip these.**

Forget generic market analysis. Most guides are obsessed with templates. Let's talk mindset. Each component matters only when you apply it correctly.

SWOT Analysis As A Superpower Detector: Coding IS NOT one of your "strength." It's the combination of your experience of going through that startup and it going right down the face — plus AI's amazing ability to crunch enormous numbers. *That's a superpower.*

The Elevator Pitch as a '*Story Spine*' – AI isn't a word generator. In reality, it is a **dopamine dealer**, disguised. It reverse engineers how people work. Pitching to seniors? Emphasize security. Beginners? Keep it stupid simple.

Financials. Your Reality Check Bodyguard.

While you are still high on launch dreams, AI asks you '*can you survive if 70% of customers ghost you?*'.

The Myth of the Solopreneur
Newsflash: Lone Wolves Die Broke
You're not alone. AI acts as your:

- **Co-Pilot.** It flags your blind spots. Like. Hey genius... Your audience has older members which you should consider. Accessibility features. Ring a bell?
- **Accountability therapist** (*"Break revenue goals into daily $37 chunks"*)
- **Mad Scientist:** Merges scattered notes into a strategy. Days 5-8 notes now make sense.

Bottom Line. Your business plan—not self-writing...yet. Planning is still work. But no more glass-chewing.

YOUR BRAND IDENTITY

Alrights. ***Brand alchemy*** is the topic at hand and AI plays its role here. Dusty old logos and taglines written by robots need to be forgotten. Actually, scratch that. Use robots while remaining the one in control of the situation.

Your brand? It's not just a logo. *It's your business's soul.* Especially if you're in AI. Your brand identity must sound smart to the outside world but it needs to communicate a human touch within it. Think ***lighthouse***. It guides lost customers. It cuts through the noise. The brand points to trust when all around you have doubts. You need to build your brand beacon particularly in an environment filled with AI tools while competing in small markets. And you need to be seen.

Why Branding Matters?

Have you ever bought from a website you had never heard off? What made you click "buy?" Design matters. **Ninety-four percent of first impressions are visual. Seventy-five percent of people judge you by looks alone.** Ouch.

AI is smart. It crunches data. It predicts trends. It writes stuff. However, AI cannot hug your customer. Not even virtually. The connection between technology products and human emotions is established through branding.

Take "*FitBot*." AI fitness coach. Mission? The mission was to "enable busy professionals to prioritize health". Not just code. It is a human problem: lack of time. Tech tool becomes real help. Boom.

THE 5 COMMANDMENTS OF AI BRANDING

Name Power.

A name is your first marketing asset. A great name sparks curiosity. They make people curious. They stick in heads. AI helps. It spits out name ideas, creative and keyword smart. Like "*Artify*" for AI art. However, would you allow it to name your firstborn? Thought not. Use AI to find initial naming ideas but veto suggestions that read like typical WiFi passwords. Here's your cheat code:

The Psychology of Naming

AI brainstorming is cool. But why do good names work? Hidden brain tricks.

- *Sound Power.* Sounds feel like things. *Kodak* and *Zappos* are sharp; sharp as K and Z. *Mom* and *Nest* are soft—M and N.
- *Brain-Friendly Names.* Cognitive Fluency. Easy to process and remember. Short names are generally easier.
- The name should create visual images in your mind. *Picture This.* "*Amazon*". Big, wild, lots of stuff.
- *Stand Out.* Different is good. In a crowded market—be weird.

AI Naming Sidekick—Not Boss.

The AI prompts in the workbook section are built to give you options. Lots of them. They use huge word banks, trend data, and competitor names. But AI is a pattern robot. It can't feel your heartbeat.

That's your job. Look at the AI names.

- *Gut Check.* Which names feel right? Like a good song.
- *Future Proof.* Can the name grow with you? Think big.
- *Trademark Check.* Is the name already taken? **Crucial step.** Check it now.
- *Say it Loud.* Easy to say? Easy to spell? Whisper it. Shout it. Would I be proud to introduce my business this way?

Names that are both meaningful and easy to discover represent the top choices.

Logo Magic

Name is the handshake, logo is the face. It's your brand's mugshot. It is, without a doubt, the most important element of any design work. Make it good.

Good logos are:
- Simple. Easy to see. Easy to recall. Even small.
- Memorable. Stands out from the crowd. Not boring.
- Timeless. Not trendy. It should be classic suit, not bell bottoms.
- Versatile. Looks good everywhere. Even on a TikTok thumbnail.
- Right Feel. Matches your brand's vibe. Serious or silly?

Core Values

Values are your business DNA. Nothing will come up with these for you. Not even AI. But AI can test them. Value: "transparency?" AI checks your website. Checks your emails. Are you walking the talk?

The AI-Human Synergy

Not long ago, establishing a professional company identity required hiring expensive agencies. Agencies charged $10,000+. Small businesses cried. Now? AI changes the game. It will be your 24/7 brand team. Fast as thought. Revolution? Not just cheap. It's fast changes. AI gives you tons of choices. Test them fast.

Use AI to iterate. Not dictate. AI is speed and quantity. Humans are meaning and quality. Come up with 50 names and ask, "Would I wear this on a T shirt?". Humans excel at meaning. Use AI to generate 10 names or 20 logo drafts. Then? Trust your gut. Less brain-fry. More heart in your brand.

Avoiding the "Robot Trap"

AI firms crash by being too cold—too fast. Brands need brains and heart. Your blockchain powered synergy is meaningless to seniors. They want clarity. "*Budget-Guardian AI*" (financial tool) is a blend of reassurance + innovation. "*Guardian*"—safe. "*AI*"—smart. Perfect.

Naming, logo creation, mission, vision, and values are not just theoretical exercises. They form the basis upon which your brand will be built and steer the entire journey of your business. A well written business plan is made up of them. Remember that these elements have subtle power as you begin to do the practical work for today.

What's Next?

Your brand is set. Now? Create offers that attract. A strong brand evolves. AI is your co-pilot. Not your autopilot.

OFFER DESIGN

"The cave you fear to enter holds the treasure you seek. "

Joseph Campbell said that.

Think about it. Starting a business is scary. Especially offer design. New entrepreneurs freeze up.

Most newbie entrepreneurs? They usually crash and burn in one of two ways.

1 One: they mimic competitors – *"Everyone sells eBooks. I'll sell eBooks!"* Sound familiar?

2 Mistake two—option paralysis. Course? Template? Coaching? Maybe a therapy llama? It's a mess.

The Real Reason People Buy
It's Not What You Think.

Fact: Your audience is *not* rational. Shocking. I know.

Not buying a list of features. Nope. They're purchasing a second, new version of themselves. Think **transformation**.

A considerate example is a retiree just starting a side hustle. Zero interest in an *"AI course"* itself. They want the result. What they want is ditch money stress and an extra $500 a month in their pockets ... without tech nightmares. That's the *real* offer. See the difference?

Think about **Apple**. Are they selling phones and laptops indeed? *Please.* **Apple** sells belonging to the cool kids' table, not circuit boards. Do they push specs? No. **Apple** sells belonging – membership in the exclusive club of cool. Status. The *"in crowd."* Circuit boards? Who cares.

Understanding how to apply the psychology of your offer comes into play here. This is about trying to reach people on the subconscious levels of desire and motivation. Ask yourself:

• What is their self-image?
• What do they wish to be and how do they see themselves?

Your offer should align with and enhance that desired self-image.

Remember. People buy with feelings. Then they use logic to justify it. Heart first. Head later. Your offer should speak to the heart first, then provide the rational reasons to support the purchase.

Pictures speak. Louder than words. *Way* louder.

Of course, you know that the human brain processes image 60,000x faster than text. Crazy fast. You don't need design skills. AI image generators are here. Turn ideas into visuals.

A grandma-friendly tax tool? Picture this—AI creates the image. Grandma beaming. Relaxed. An AI avatar diligently files her taxes. Easy. Trustworthy.

Visuals help YOU too. Not just for customers. They solidify your own vision. Abstract ideas? Suddenly—tangible. Doable.

AI Stops You Overcomplicating

Sure. AI can build a spaceship. But its real power? Forcing simplicity. A beginner's offer suite should balance aspiration with practicality. Use AI prompts like:

• "Identify the most common technical barriers for MY AUDIENCE when using MY PRODUCT TYPE"
• "Generate a list of 'good, better, best' pricing tiers for MY AUDIENCE with THIS BUDGET RANGE"
• "Give me pricing tiers for [audience] who think 'ROI' is a typo"

This way you can prevent yourself from dealing with artificial problems by ensuring your solutions address genuine business concerns. Not invented from a 2 am brainstorming.

In the world of online business, the most successful entrepreneurs rarely rely on just one product or service. What they do instead is creating a product suite or a value ladder. Different offers at different prices. Using AI assistance makes suite creation both simpler and more effective.

Think about it. Brands you admire. Multiple offers **ALWAYS**. Free content to platinum packages. Not random at all. They understand that customers are diverse. Different needs. Different bank accounts. Different levels of trust (initially).

The ultimate sales hack? Make your offers a journey. One offer smoothly leads to the next. Value ladder in action. Serve customers at every stage of their needs. Boost your income big time.

This creates multiple income streams from the SAME customer base. It is a thousand times easier to sell to happy customers than chasing a stranger. A good offer suite can triple your customer value. Maybe even five times more. Seriously.

If you are planning to use AI to design your product suite, aim to find out the whole journey that your ideal customer needs to take. What's their first struggle? What comes next? What's their ultimate goal? AI refines your message. Makes your offer appear as alluring. Less like a sales pitch. More like a **Hell yes. Where's the buy button?**

In the next section, we will see how to place these offers in a saturated market, converting curiosity into commitment.

ART OF WAR—AI EDITION: BUSINESS IS WAR. WITHOUT THE SWORDS (MOSTLY).

88% of startups fail from poor market reading—not bad ideas. You could have a genius product but without battlefield awareness, you are fighting the drone war with a butter knife.

If Sun Tzu Had an AI Assistant

You have brainstormed a strong offer suite, the vision of what you will bring to the market. But a product, no matter how groundbreaking, exists in a real world. A battlefield, if you will. It's important to understand this battlefield, and surprisingly, **Sun Tzu's ancient wisdom is perfectly in line with the power of modern AI.**

Sun Tzu's terrain? Your market. Here's how to conquer it:

Your Market Realities Take Precedence Over Concepts Alone

Great generals didn't win on muscle. They studied terrain. Also, by knowing enemies and weather. In business, your "terrain" is threefold:

Market Size: Gold Mine or Ghost Town?

A small piece of a massive market beats dominating a tiny one, every single time. But it's not enough to know the current size. What's the growth trajectory? Is this worth your life savings?

A pro tip for most beginners: A market with a billion dollar potential is useless if 90% is already locked down by the established players.

Competitive Intelligence

There are countless companies scattered around the business graveyard that underestimated their rivals. And competitor analysis is not an obsession with rivals; instead, it is an opportunity to learn from the rivals. Their strengths show what customers value. Weaknesses show opportunities. Their pricing? Sets market expectations. What your shared audience responds to is shown in their marketing.

Tools like ***Visualping? Think AI spyglass.*** It watches competitor websites, marks changes and spits out summaries. Boom.

Visualping Features: You set the watch intervals. Catches visual and text changes. AI summaries – the works.

Visualping Benefits: Competitor website monitoring. AI alerts. Know competitor strategies. See market shifts coming.

This includes new emerging trends & regulations that you will not want to be blindsided by.

Most importantly, technology especially AI is a moving target. Could there be fundamentally new trends that could affect your market for the better or for the worse? What about the legal stuff? Do you know whether there are regulations concerning your niche with regards to AI? You must expect these things.

Here are several organizations that effectively handle these matters.

◦ **Apple Inc.—Strategic Launch God.**

Apple? Textbook strategic marketing. Apple dominates product launches. Their product launches are legendary, not by accident, but by design. Pure strategy.

They create anticipation with marketing. Genius. Teasers from months before, leaks in the months before, buzz before the launch. Excitement overload.

Timed Release Cycles. Perfect timing. Key shopping seasons. Products ready right after announcement.

◦ **Coca-Cola: Excels in budget allocation.**

Coca-Cola—brand stays number one globally. How? Relentless global ad spend. Constant cash flow.

Coke ads are global. TV. Web. Sponsors. Outdoor signs. Everywhere.

Channel Choices. Budget spread wide. Attacks every channel to the fullest to hit their reach and engagement. Max reach. Max eyes.

Example.

Suppose, your AI dog walking service is to be pitched to investors. You walk in. Grab the marker. And boom. Dogs require fresh outdoor experience more than smartphone apps. That's your hook. Now, let's talk business.

Target Market—Your Doggone Good Customers

You have instincts regarding your target customer. Time to nail it down:

- **Demographics.** Gen Z men who are fathers of dogs also need to manage their Zoom calls at work. Retirees? Spoiling their grand-pups? Who are they really?

- **Psychographics.** Eco-warriors? Wanting carbon-neutral walks? Luxury hounds? Demanding gold leashes? (Yep, gold leashes are real.) What drives them?
- **Needs.** What's the dog walk struggle? Crazy schedules? Safety worries? Just plain don't-want-to? What problem are you solving?
- **Market Size.** 63 million US dog owners. Each spending over $1,300 a year on pets. Do the math. Big numbers.
- **Growth Trends.** More dog owners? How much additional money is being spent on their pet dogs? Is this market up to a point where we can begin investing again?
- **Future Projections.** Will dog walking emerge as the following massive business opportunity? Prove it with data. Don't just guess.

Competition. Who Else is Chasing Tails?

Who are they? List them. Apps... Local walkers... Even the kid next door. Everyone's competition.

- **Strengths.** They excel at these specific parts of their business model. Low prices? Rave reviews? Catchy jingles? What works for them?
- **Weaknesses.** Where are they vulnerable to the attacks of the enemy? Limited hours? No tech? Grumpy walker vibes? Where can you beat them?

Industry Trends. Sniffing Out the Future.

- **Emerging Tech.** Robot dogs? Self-walking? Coming for your job? What's changing the game?
- **Consumer Habits.** Do users eliminate app subscriptions in favor of purchasing personal walking devices? Are dog services being asked to deliver more? What do customers want now?
- **Economic Factors.** Are dog owners in for a recession hit on the wallet? Leashes tightening? How will the economy bite?

Analyze your market. Tell the investors you're not running after your tail. You're leading the pack.

As Sun Tzu put it:

"Victorious warriors win first then go to war."

Your move—General of the Dog Walkers.

· · ·

Alright! For a second, forget about having the world's greatest offer. Seriously. Take the world's greatest offer, and without the right roadmap? You are revving a *Ferrari* in a garage. Here's a gut punch. The data consistently shows that acquiring new customers costs *5-25 times more than retaining existing ones*. Let that sink in. Your marketing strategy is the *GPS*. Avoids those costly detours.

WHY YOUR CUSTOMER'S BRAIN IS A MAZE (NOT A HIGHWAY)

Every customer's journey is a story. When was the last purchase of an expensive item you made? Pure logic? Doubt it. Emotions? Chances are, it was a combination of both. Customers don't wake up craving purchases—they trip into them through problems. They stumble into purchases while trying to solve problems. Traditional marketing? Thinks linear. AI shows it's a maze. Picture a retiree. Researching AI tools for ads? Starts on *Google*. Then a *YouTube* rabbit hole. Ends up on *Reddit* seeking approval. Ring a bell?

CHANNELS THAT ACTUALLY WORK

Marketing channels? Not slot machines to gamble on. Think ecosystems. Gen Z would fall for a viral *TikTok* dance, yes. But your grandma? She's trusting email newsletters or her *Facebook* groups. AI? You can consider it as your *cultural translator*. It processes data about the demographics and engagement. It identifies where your audience really spends time.

Consider this. For example, an AI tool might show that queries in *Reddit's r/side-hustle* about 'AI for passive income' are mostly from beginners looking for step by step guides. Meanwhile, *LinkedIn* is preferred among semi-retired professionals. Now? You are deploying your resources exactly where the target audience will receive maximum benefit.

The true factors behind how buyers decide is where AI provides unmatched knowledge. Forget snapshots of customer behavior. AI gives us the entire motion picture.

THE 3 PSYCHOLOGICAL TRIGGERS AI MASTERS

- *Reciprocity*: Give value before asking for the sale. People naturally want to return the favor. Think content marketing. Think free trials.
- *Scarcity*. Limited-time offers. Yeah, they work. Our brains have a strong reaction to the fear of missing out. AI? It identifies how best to present limited-time deals at their optimal moment.
- *Social proof*: Testimonials? Not just fluff. We're herd animals. Show us the crowd is going in that direction. We'll follow.

In this context, AI is what makes it revolutionary because it allows you to scale these psychological triggers. Your AI system helps you make unique journeys that match how each lead approaches buying decisions.

Look at ***Netflix***. ***Netflix*** didn't beat ***Blockbuster*** by luck. As they moved from DVD rentals to streaming, they didn't simply deploy a platform and wait for subscribers on top. They analyzed viewing habits. Leveraged social proof. Personalized recommendations. This was marketing and product development – a perfect team.

THE FIVE PILLARS OF AN UNBEATABLE GAME PLAN

- ***Customer Understanding***: Know their pain points better than their own therapist. Seriously.
- ***Channel Selection***: Fish where the fish are actually biting
- ○ ***LinkedIn***? ***TikTok***? Hell, maybe even snail mail.
- ***Message Clarity***. Attempts at speaking about everything will lead to complete message confusion. *Say Everything. Say Nothing.*
- ***Conversion Architecture***. The Funnel. Yeah, it's still a thing. Make it easy to buy.
- ***Measurement Framework***. What gets measured does get improved.

AI's real magic in marketing? **Automation**. And **personalization**. The ultimate power couple. Old-school marketing? It forced you to decide, high touch, tiny scale personal service or low touch, massive scale mass marketing. AI? Kills that false choice.

Look at ***Amazon***. They personalize shopping. ***FOR MILLIONS***. Simultaneously! Every visitor sees tailored recommendations. Automated. Yet incredibly personal.

Modern companies of all sizes now benefit from this technology. Not just tech giants. YOU can do this.

We'll see in the next section how AI can help you when it comes to setting up very realistic as well as insightful financial forecasts... *Spoiler*. It's not as "spreadsheet hell' as it is 'chess master meets CFO."

FINANCIAL FORECASTING

AI startups? Love to self-destruct. Their weapon of choice? Ignoring the money math. Let's stop the madness.

The time has come for us to step into what is usually one of the most crucial but, unfortunately, the most overlooked zones in our AI business plan: ***Financial Forecasting***. You have an exceptional AI solution. But will it be a business? ***Financial forecasting? Critical.*** It determines sustainable success.

When entrepreneurs start making money guesses, they usually fall into two comedy categories—*Looney Tunes* optimism or *Eeyore* pessimism.

Happy founders dream of hockey stick growth. Customers line up day one in their dreams. Wallets wide open. Pessimists, burned before, are too conservative. They kill potentially lucrative opportunities. Both are wrong, obviously. But, the optimist at least enjoys the ride. So the optimist wins in this regard.

Many people overlook this fact that business forecasting is more than just mathematical calculations because it needs to convey its message through stories. The story your numbers should tell is that the hero (you) doesn't die in chapter three. It has to convince YOU and potential backers.

AI is a curveball for forecasts. Old rules don't quite fit. Low start-up costs. Deceptive. Early profits seem easy. *Dangerously easy.*

THE THREE FINANCIAL HORIZONS OF AI VENTURES

AI's Three Money Zones

Think of AI business in three stages. Like levels in a game.

First – **Development Horizon.** You build. No money in. Money out. Lots of it. Development costs. Data costs. Training costs. This period is about survival and reaching a viable product.

Next? **Market Validation Horizon.** Product is live. Revenue starts appearing but grows slowly. You tweak the product. Find customers. Reality hits hard here. Optimism fades. You have reached the point of disillusionment with your current venture. Many *QUIT* here. **YOU WON'T!**

Then – **Scaling Horizon.** AI magic time. Tech is set. Growth explodes. Costs stay low. Money picture changes fast. From scary to amazing.

The Three Pillars of Sane Forecasting—AI Style
Revenue: Money Rivers Not Streams

Money comes in many ways. Not just one pipe. AI helps map these rivers.

Market tides. The market wave shows if your product field expands or contracts. Within one coffee break AI checks 100 industry reports.

Pricing alchemy. Your business offers multiple price options between basic and premium plans to capture customers of different spending levels.

Customer pool size. Pond or ocean of customers? AI estimates your total market (*TAM*). It spots crowded niches. Avoid those.

Pro Tip: recurrent revenue is oftentimes forgotten by the newbies. AI can find subscription models. Making one time buyers, loyal customers.

Expenses: The Silent Killer

Dreams die here. Hidden costs win. Bakery fails not from bad bread. It fails because the owner forgot equipment repairs. For AI, watch out for:

- Regular AI tool expenses of $20 per month will build up quickly into large payments.
- Your expenses for AI hosting will increase quickly as your user numbers expand by 10 times.
- Human cleanup crews for AI's occasional "creative" outputs

AI is your expense detective. It sees expense patterns in other companies. Learn from their pain. Consider it financial early warning system.

Funding. Bootstrap or Beg for Cash? Decide Smart.

Not always necessary. AI can help you decide:

- If you're either making more revenue than expense in the first 12 months, this will be the **Bootstrap Zone.**
- If you expect it to take 6-18 months to get your breakeven point, microloans or grants can help to fill in the gap.
- Moonshot. Building the next Uber? Venture capital might be needed. However, you will have to lose some control.

Ok. Let's move on. ***Sensitivity Analysis. Mostly overlooked.***

It's a simulator. For hypotheticals.

Here's the core idea:

First, determine the key variables or most important assumptions for your revenue and expenses. These might include:

- Customer Cost (CAC): Cost to obtaining one customer.
- Conversion Rate: Lookers to buyers ratio?
- Average Money Per User ($ARPU$): How much money per customer on average?
- Percentage of Customers lost each month (Churn Rate)?
- Pricing. Will affect how much people want to buy and how much money you will make.
- Key Expense Categories. See How Your Business Performance Changes when You Shift Marketing or IT Spending and Worker Wages

Create Scenarios.

Analyze the Impact: Now run key financial metrics (revenue, expenses, profit, cash flow) for each scenario in order to trigger 'break even' in at least one of them. Find out how sensitive your business is.

Sensitivity Analysis identifies Risks: Helps you in identifying your weak spots. Small change in customer cost kills profit? You know to focus on customer acquisition.

AI's Role. You will be using AI to aid the initial projections generation. Sensitivity analysis tests it. AI models scenarios. You make sense of them. AI predicts data. You make it meaningful. *Human brain still needed.*

The Rule of Three in Money Forecasts

The *"Rule of Three"* is a term that I use to describe the process often used by professional investors and experienced entrepreneurs in financial planning.

The first thing you want to do is to create your best case forecast on reasonable assumptions.

Second, double your expected timeline to significant revenue.

Third, triple your anticipated expenses.

Not pessimism—pragmatism. Research backs it up—entrepreneurs always underestimate costs and overestimate revenue speed. The Rule of Three? The Rule of Three is a safety net. The Rule of Three is a buffer that saves businesses.

A forecast is just a story. Until money hits the bank. Make yours a page-turner.

Money compass set right? Good. Next—your toolkit. Or your team. Best plan needs right tools and people. *Execution is everything.*

TEAM DYNAMICS IN THE AI ERA

Why 5 People Now Beat 50

"Less is more." Instagram sold for a cool billion with just 13 people. WhatsApp? 450 million users – with only 55 employees. Mind. Blown. These were not accidents. They were previews. **A new reality is here.** Few team members can now outperform large staff organizations thanks to AI technology. Forget penny-pinching. *This is about rewriting business itself.*

The "Solo Maestro" Playbook

Minimum Viable Team is the new *Minimum Viable Product*. Smallest group possible to nail your vision without stepping on each other's toes. For solopreneurs? You are now a "team of one plus AI."

People are wrong when they claim that AI kills human jobs; AI enhances human power. Fills in your weaknesses. Yet that will work only if you ruthlessly clarify the make up of your team (or solo role).

The Four Critical Human Roles in Any AI Business

Automation is strong. *Humans are still king (or queen).* Great AI businesses keep humans in these four areas:

- **Where are we going?** Someone must decide. AI suggests routes. Human judgment decides the business's direction. *Business direction needs human leadership. Strategic direction. Human job.*
- **Customer Connection:** Real customer love is human. AI reads feedback. Humans understand feelings that build loyalty.
- **Problems? Bring humans.** AI finds patterns. Humans make leaps of insight when it is required. *Lateral thinking—human domain.*
- **Be good. Not just rich. *Ethical Guardian:*** AI has no conscience. Humans do. Ethics matter. Humans ensure ethical business practices. Profit isn't everything. *Ethical oversight—human job.*

Team or no team – these four need human attention.

The Solopreneur Advantage

Solopreneurs? Reaching 7 figures? Not a myth. These are individuals making seven figures – without employees. They succeed by:

- *Force Multiplier Tools.* They use tools that make their individual efforts explode.
- It means developing deep expertise in a certain field.
- Systems which automatically scale up operations without needing more human staff
- They partner strategically instead of hiring.
- They have to maintain exceptional focus on high value activities

Big money. Low risk. Perfect for freedom seekers who hate office politics.

Hybrid Models

The Best of Both Worlds

A complete range of business structures exists between fully staffed businesses and self-operated businesses. Successful online entrepreneurs, however, normally have a really small "core team" handling critical functions and leverage freelancers, automation and strategic partnerships for anything else.

This allows flexibility. For the larger projects you can scale up resources, and then scale down resources minimising ongoing costs. It offers the benefits of a team with a support and specialization without the fixed overhead of a typical employment model.

Beyond Job Titles

Strategic Role Mapping

Even a one person operation needs roles, not just tasks. Between being the "Chief Storyteller" and the "Data Alchemist" a solopreneur handles two roles while small teams assign specific roles "AI Prompt Engineer" and "Customer Whisperer" along with others. **The key? You should establish roles according to what outcomes each position achieves regardless of working hours.**

Example: AI children's book creator? The company requires someone to be the "Narrative Architect" for story ideas alongside another person who functions as the "Visual Wizard" to enhance AI art. Even if it's you doing both. Naming the roles forces precision.

Once roles are well distinguished, you will see where your skills are strong and where reinforcements are needed.

Skill Gap Analysis

No one excels at everything. Beginners tend to overestimate themselves especially when it comes to their capacity ("I'm just going to learn coding!"). Seniors might underestimate their skills. "I cannot adapt to social media because of my age." Your abilities need an objective evaluation through AI systems.

Ask:

"What skills are *non negotiable* for YOUR BUSINESS?"

Compare: Your current skills to that list.

Pro Tip. Whenever there is a gap in your company it provides an open space for new innovative solutions. Can you automate the gap? Partner? Outsource?

This leads us to an important question to address. Build, borrow, or buy talent?

Team Architecture. Outsourcing vs. In-House

Freelancers are flexible. Employees provide consistency. Your time becomes more productive through virtual assistants which manage repetitive work as they help you complete important projects.

Example: An AI writer drafts blogs. A human editor adds the spark.

Customer service. Chatbots resolve 80% of queries and the rest requiring empathy is taken care of by you.

However, before you actually onboard anyone, there is one non negotiable step...

LEGAL SAFEGUARDS. *THE BORING STUFF.*

The law even applies to AI businesses. Licensing. Data privacy. Contracts. These protect you. AI can help. Try prompts like:

> *Create a compliance checklist for businesses in YOUR SECTOR that operates in YOUR LOCALITY.*

WARNING: Human lawyer review is essential. AI informs. Humans make the final decisions.

Visualizing Success.

Think about your venture at its peak. Solo founder? Orchestrating AI tools? A war room of a virtual team brainstorming? Create a vision board (even mentally).

Your team? It's not about headcount. **It's about leverage.** AI's the ultimate intern. Works 24/7. Never sleeps. Doesn't steal your lunch.

The next item on your business plan is your executive summary; the final piece of your business plan and the last thing to settle. This is not a summary, it's your final pitch as you put all that you have designed into a story that will impress investors, customers and your future self...

THE EXECUTIVE SUMMARY

Today, we went through a lot of territory. We are now at that final and essential step of condensing all that effort down into its most concentrated form: the ***executive summary***.

> *"The biggest enemy of communication is the illusion of communication."* — *George Bernard Shaw.*

Think about that. Your executive summary? It is fighting for attention in a world of illusions.

Attention spans are brutal. Average business brain? **8-second attention span.** Eight seconds. Business pros? Goldfish territory. It is known as the *'attention economy'* to the psychologists. The reason why isn't that people are getting less intelligent, it's an adaptive response to information overwhelm.

For your AI business, that means your executive summary has **ONE** job in those first few seconds: ***Hook. Trigger. Credibility.*** Most founders get this totally backwards. They lead with credentials not the *why*. Tech details? Nope. Lead with *"why."* The reason you exist.

Direct messages need to grab attention without losing excitement. In a concise summary, you can (and should) inject elements of storytelling. Human beings automatically respond to narrative patterns. Think about the examples in the workbook, the ***"Spotify, but for workouts"***, it is very easy to visualize.

First Impressions

The human brain processes information in seconds. A weak opener? You've lost them. Here's the twist. AI isn't just your tool. It's your audience's expectation. Investors now look for AI-native information through bullet-pointed reports that use facts to explain high-value specifics. Your one-sentence pitch? A ***"neural hook."*** It skips skepticism and lodges in memory. For example, Airbnb did not say, "We rent rooms." Their message? ***Book unique homes. Book unique experiences. Just like a local.***

Less Really IS More

Great summaries withhold information—on purpose. The summary should not be a miniature version of your business plan but rather a teaser trailer to a blockbuster movie.

This is backed up by *Harvard Business School* studies. A ***"curiosity gap"*** is what ideal summary creates. The gap between their knowledge and the knowledge that they lack. Irresistible pull.

For AI businesses in particular. Be crystal clear as to what the problem is. Skip the discussion of algorithms in technical jargon. What the market buys is solutions, not technology.

Tomorrow? We're *Storming the Castle*

Book III drops the theory and loads the cannons: ***"The Easiest Route to Passive Income with AI".*** Digital products are the target. Product creation. Marketing. Operations. The works. Starting with in-depth keyword and market research for max profit and visibility.

Today—executive summary mastered. Your initial high-level business document has developed into an optimized executive summary. Your ability to narrow your vision into a compelling story with attention-grabbing elements is now fully developed. Now, action time. Workbook out. Entrepreneurial espresso brewing. Compelling pitch to build. Activities waiting to turn your plan into irresistible opportunity. Let's work.

KEY TAKEAWAYS

- ***The stone age has ended for business plans. AI Transforms Business Plans.*** Old business plans operate at a slow and painful pace. AI injects fun and smarts. **Level up or get left behind.**
- ***Fear is the Enemy. AI is the Exorcist.*** Planning paralysis? AI offers instant feedback. **No more excuses.**

- ***SWOT meets AI.*** Ditch boring analysis.
- ***Solopreneur? Meet Your AI Co-Pilot.*** Lone wolves die broke.
- ***Brand Soul, Not Robot Shell.*** AI brands need heart. Smart and human.
- ***Logo Face, Not Just Scribble.*** Simple, memorable, timeless. Your brand's mugshot. **Make it count.**
- At the core of every successful offer exists a transformation which delivers concrete outcomes to people. Don't copy the herd. Dodge option paralysis. Forget feature lists. The new identity consumers want to see must be your main selling point.
- ***Visuals grab brains. AI image gen? Your new best friend.*** **Show, don't just tell.**
- ***Overthinking? Rookie mistake. Simplicity Wins. AI? Forces It.*** Focus on real problems. Real solutions.
- Offer a ladder of products and the customer will walk it (product suite is key). Don't just sell one thing. Serve customers at every need.
- ***Sun Tzu in tandem with AI brings a wartime perspective to the world of business. Market = Battlefield. AI = Sun Tzu.*** A lack of market understanding results in business failure. **Conquer or crumble.**
- AI Tools provide business intelligence through ethical monitoring of competitor moves. **Stay ahead. Don't be blindsided.**
- **Know Your Customers.** *Deeper than they know themselves.* **Nail it or fail it.**
- ***Marketing GPS beats Ferrari in a garage.*** Customers stumble into purchases. Use psychology.
- ***Financials with AI. Sanity Check. Not Spreadsheet Hell.*** AI helps you face reality. ***Rule of Three.*** Double time, triple costs. Business owners typically predict expenses to be lower while anticipating their launch speeds to be faster than they actually end up being. As your safety mechanism for practical planning you should use the ***Rule of Three.***
- ***Small Team, Big Impact.*** The messaging platform WhatsApp operated with only 55 staff members to serve 450 million users. AI Multiplies. Less is the new more.
- ***Human Roles Still Rule.*** AI assists, doesn't replace. Humans for direction, connection, problems, ethics. AI for everything else.
- ***Executive Summary. Hook in 8 Seconds.*** Goldfish attention spans. Lead with "why," not "what." Tease them. Don't spill the beans. ***Curiosity Gap. Leave Them Wanting More.*** A great summary creates intrigue.
- **Boom. Go get 'em.**

Day 9: WORKBOOK

T*he Brand DNA Lab*

Activity 1: Story Archetype Discovery (Human-Centered)

Some brands feel like family. Ever wondered why? Blame ***Carl Jung***. Great brands connect. How? ***Archetypes***. Jung knew his stuff—fundamental character patterns. So, your mission is to take the *30 seconds quiz* [here], crack your brand's core personality.

This quizz will help you find your archetype. Scan the QR code or visit this link below to access the quizz. Type out the entire url including "https://".

`https://go.yspweb.com/brand-archetype-quiz`

A I Prompt
Archetype Expansion

Your expertise in brand strategy should include complete mastery of **Jungian archetypes**. I chose the **[YOUR ARCHETYPE]** brand because it matches the needs of people who want to **[FIRST BLANK]** while requiring **[SECOND BLANK]** to achieve **[THIRD BLANK]**. Based on this:

1 Give 3-5 key personality traits that my brand should have.

2 Create 3 storytelling themes that will appeal to my audience

3 Identify potential pitfalls or shadow aspects of this archetype I should avoid

4 Recommend one unexpected way to express this archetype that would stand out in my market

ACTIVITY 2: EMOTIONAL WIRING KIT

Human + AI Hybrid

Newsflash! People buy *feelings*. Not features.

Step 1. Choose 3 primary emotions. Your brand interaction should evoke these in your audience.

• Security/Trust
• Joy/Happiness
• Hope/Optimism
• Relief/Comfort
• Belonging/Connection
• Achievement/Pride
• Wonder/Discovery
• Confidence

Step 2: Write a personal experience (2-3 sentences) for each emotion in the form of a story that encapsulates this emotion.

AI Prompt

You know that you are an emotional branding expert. For my brand, I want to create a sensation of **[EMOTION 1]**, **[EMOTION 2]** and **[EMOTION 3]**. Here are personal stories:

[PASTE YOUR STORIES]

Based on these stories:

1 I need to identify the essential emotional triggers which will help me build my brand messaging.

2 Suggest ways in which one could bring about these emotions practically through:

  ◦ Customer interaction points
  ◦ Visual elements

° Language patterns

3 Emotion journey—map it out. Awareness to loyalty—how do these feelings flow?

4 Provide recommendations on metrics to see if I am achieving these emotional connections.

ACTIVITY 3: VISUAL IDENTITY HEIST

AI-Assisted

As you all know, visual elements can be used as mighty communicators of a brand. This exercise uses AI to convert emotion insights into visual language.

Step 1. Create a simple mood board. List the following items.

• 3 colors—brand emotions in color code.

• Two textures or patterns that should reflect your brand personality

• 3 objects—brand purpose in symbol form.

• 1 natural element—brand energy—water—fire—earth—air—choose your element.

AI Prompt

These are the elements of the brand identity I'm making.
• Colors: **[YOUR COLORS]**
• Textures/patterns: [...]
• Symbolic objects: [...]
• Natural element: [...]
• Brand archetype: [...]
• Primary emotions: [...]
Please generate:

1 A color palette. *Hex codes.*

2 3 logo concept descriptions (not images) that incorporate my symbolic elements

3 Typography. Header font. Body font.

4 Design principles. **Stay consistent.**

AI Prompt - Logo Visualization:

In accordance with this logo concept, **[PASTE YOUR FAVORITE LOGO CONCEPT]**
Make a simple logo that contains:
• My brand archetype. **[YOUR ARCHETYPE]**
• Core emotions. **[YOUR EMOTIONS]**
• Key colors. **[YOUR COLORS]**
• This symbolic element. **[CHOOSE ONE SYMBOL]**

ACTIVITY 4: VOICE KARAOKE NIGHT

Human + AI Collaboration

Your brand's voice? How it speaks to the world. As an adaptation of the widely known *'Karaoke Exercise'* used by top agencies, this exercise assists in establishing a brand voice that is genuine and consistent. It is not about singing, do not worry.

Step 1. Pick a song that *is* your brand, if it could belt out a tune. Why this song? What brand qualities does it scream?

Step 2: Write a 30–50 word welcome message for a new customer as if you're your brand.

AI Prompt:

> The song that represents my brand voice is **[SONG NAME]** because **[YOUR REASON]**. These are the qualities it has: **[QUALITIES]**.
> My brand welcomes new customers through this message:
> **[YOUR WELCOME MESSAGE]**
> For my brand voice please:
> 1 Analyze my welcome message and extract 5 voice characteristics
> 2 Create a brand voice chart with the two columns of "We are" and "We are not"
> 3 Welcome message—rewrite—subtly better. Authenticity—untouched.
> 4 Generate 3 more voice examples:
> ° Social media post (new product).
> ° A response to a customer complaint
> ° Thank you email once a purchase is made

BRAND DNA INTEGRATION EXERCISE (THE GRAND FINALE)

Time to synthesize. One document. Your brand's DNA.

AI Prompt - Brand DNA Synthesizer:

> So the results of completing the Brand DNA Lab exercises are as follows.
> • Archetype. **[YOUR ARCHETYPE]**
> • Core emotions. **[YOUR EMOTIONS]**
> • Visual elements. **[KEY VISUAL ELEMENTS]**
> • Voice characteristics. **[VOICE QUALITIES]**
> Please create a one-page Brand DNA document that integrates all these elements into a brand name. Also provide the following.
> • No corporate word salad positioning statement.
> • 3 rules to prevent brand schizophrenia
> • An origin story *Marvel* would steal
> • Real reasons I'll crush competitors

In 4 steps you have just built a bulletproof identity. **What's your excuse now?**

ACTIVITY OVERVIEW

Alan Lakein's quote is *"failing to plan is planning to fail."* Don't let that be you.
You will create three things:
- *Financial forecasts.*
- *A team plan built for strength.*
   ○ Yes. AI counts as "staff".
- *Legal protections so tight that a lawyer would approve.*

Your will need : Google Sheets, a coffee and your favorite AI assistant. Let's roll.

Section 1: Your *No-BS* Financial Forecast

Step 1. Fire up Sheets

Free. Simple. Your new financial war room.

Step 2.

Open that spreadsheet and create three sections:
- 0-12 months
- 13-24 months
- Scaling Horizon (25-36 months)

AI Prompt:

> I am developing financial projections for an idea I want to launch [provide brief details about your business plan]. Forecast for three phases: Develop (0-12 months). Validate (13-24 months). Scale (25-36 months). Realistic milestones. Money targets. Expenses. Give it to me straight.

Step 3. Apply the famous ***Rule of Three***.

Plan for the unexpected. Create three scenarios for each time horizon:
- Baseline: What you expect.
- Timeline Scenario: Double the timeline to hit those revenue targets. ***Ouch.***
- Expense Scenario: Expenses are three times higher than anticipated. ***Double ouch.***

AI Prompt for Rule of Three Application:

> I have created a baseline financial forecast for my AI business with [X revenue and Y expenses] in the first year. Give me two more scenarios: 1) Revenue takes twice as long to materialize. 2) Expenses are three times higher than I planned.
> For each, how much extra funding do I need to break even?

Next step

Determine the variables that have biggest impact on your business success. Common ones include:

- Cost to acquire a Customer
- Conversion Rate—Lookers to buyers—the magic ratio.
- Average Revenue Per User (ARPU)—Money per customer—the revenue engine.
- Churn Rate

AI Prompt Drill #3 – Weakness Exposure:

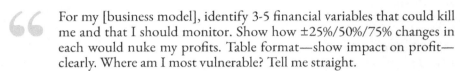

> For my [business model], identify 3-5 financial variables that could kill me and that I should monitor. Show how ±25%/50%/75% changes in each would nuke my profits. Table format—show impact on profit—clearly. Where am I most vulnerable? Tell me straight.

Section 2: Strategic Team Architecture

Step 1. Choose one of these tools for mapping

Tool Options:
- Miro (free tier available)
- Lucidchart (free tier available)
- Draw.io (completely free)

Step 2: The Four Pillars of Business

Four *non-negotiable* functions:
- Business Direction. That's you, visionary
- Customer Connection. AI chatbots need not apply. *Yet!*
- Problem Solving
- Ethical Oversight (Avoid becoming a Twitter scandal)

AI Prompt for Role Definition:

> For my [niche] AI biz, define responsibilities and tools for Business Direction, Customer Connection, Problem Solving, Ethical Oversight. Please suggest which tools or AI capabilities can be used to improve performance of each of the functions.

Step 3: Conduct a Skills Autopsy

AI Prompt Drill #5 – Skills Inventory:

> An AI business focused on [your specific idea] needs to develop a skills checklist. Include: 1) Essential skills to run this thing successfully. 2) A rating scale, please (be honest!), 1 to 5. 3) Skills to keep in house versus those to outsource. 4) AI tools to plug the holes.
>
> Please format this as a skills matrix I can use to honestly assess my capabilities.

Step 4. Your Team Architecture

Using the skills gap analysis results make strategic decisions:
- Which functions will you personally handle?
- Where do you need human partners?

- What are the functions that are possible to automate with AI?
- What should be outsourced to specialists?

AI Prompt for Team Architecture Planning:

> AI—Skills assessment. Strengths—[your strengths]. Weaknesses—[your weaknesses]. Recommend team architecture for my AI business —bootstrap mode—budget tight.
>   1 Core functions I should personally handle
>   2 Functions needing hires or partners.
>   3 Functions automatable with AI (suggest tools!).
>   4 Functions for outsourcing—best options.

Section 3. Legalities.
Step 1: Legal Landmines – Requirements Identification
Tool Options:
- A chatbot
- Some legal prompt engineering

Step 2: Compliance Checklist
Time to get legally legit.

AI Prompt Drill #7 – Legal Compliance Checklist:

> I have launched my AI activities within [your AI service] at [location]. List all legal requirements: biz registration, GDPR/CCPA, IP protections, contracts, taxes. Explain each item and give a resource.

Step 3. Draft Legal Documents
AI Prompt Drill #8 – Legal Template Factory:

> AI—Templates for my AI business [brief description].
>   1 A privacy policy which follows official privacy protection laws
>   2 Terms of service agreement—template.
>   3 Client/customer contract template
>   4 Intellectual property protection statement—template.
>   5 Data processing agreement—template.
>   Please note that these will be starting templates that need review by a qualified attorney.

Step 4: Human Legal Review Plan
Research review options that are affordable.

Congratulations! You're Now *Fortress Certified*
You've got:
- Legal docs.
- Financial plans. For three apocalypses.
- A combined team made up of 50% humans and 50% AI, but *100% functional*.

THE AI PITCH WORKSHOP

Imagine your complicated AI business idea and retelling it in a manner that leaves an impact on anyone you talk to and actually brings results.

Ready to make that happen?

Activity 1: Story Surgery—Business Plan Edition.

Duration: 30 minutes

Step 1. Core Elements.

You want to extract these key elements from your business plan.

The Problem that keeps your audience awake at 3 AM

☐ Problem: _____

Your magic trick. How do you fix that headache? Keep it simple.

☐ Solution: _____

The people in the **Target Market** willing to tattoo your logo on their arm

☐ Target Market: _____

The **UVP** that makes competitors sweat

☐ Unique Value: _____

A set of **Metrics** accountants will weep with joy over

☐ Key Metrics: _____

Step 2: Story Arc Development

• Beginning (Hook): _____

• Middle (Challenge): _____

• End (Resolution): _____

Example: "Marketers waste 12 weekly hours to content – *RealFreshCopy.ai* Our AI slashes that to 15 minutes. Do you want to know how 100,000 teams are acquiring 48 extra days a year?"

Activity 2: Hook Creation Workshop 🎙 Duration: 20 minutes

Your opener should have as much caffeine as espresso, not lukewarm tea.

The AI prompt here is "I want five opening lines for [solution] that results in [audience] spitting out their coffee when they hear [problem] gets resolved"

Example Hooks

Steal These:

"Imagine. Anticipating customer needs? Before they even arise?"

"Imagine. Cutting time waste in creating content. By 80%? While doubling engagement?"

"Three years ago, we lost a cool million to poor data quality. Nowadays, we save companies ten million."

Activity 3: The Curiosity Gap Exercise

Duration: 20 minutes

Formula:

• Tell an eye raising stat such as "30% of marketing budgets disappear into thin air..."

• Twist the knife. "But what if... You could claw that back?"

• Reveal the solution

Template. "Did you know? This [industry problem]. Costs businesses [amount]? Our solution enables businesses to achieve [hint at benefit] through its features."

Example: "Did you know? The average business loses thirty percent of its marketing budget because of ineffective targeting methods. Our AI platform helps companies recover that lost revenue by..."

Activity 4: The One-Line Money Maker (20 min)
Elevator's about to hit the ground floor. You've got seconds. Make. It. Count.

Recipe:
[Name] assists [audience] to get rid off [pain] with [secret sauce] and get [orgasmic outcome].

Template:
- Company Name: _____
- Target Audience: _____
- Problem: _____
- Solution: _____
- Key Benefit: _____

Evaluation Checklist ✅
Rate each component 1-5:
☐ Problem Clarity?
☐ Memorability of your hook?
☐ Effectiveness of that curiosity gap?
☐ Conciseness of your one-sentence pitch?
☐ Story flow smoother than a jazz solo

AI Assistant Prompts 👑
- For Story Development: "The business elements will be turned into an interesting story with real world impact: [paste your business elements]".
  - Hook Limp? → "Make this benefit sound like free cocaine: [technical term]"
- For Curiosity Gap: Build a curiosity generating statement on [key metric or benefit], so that the reader would like to learn more about it
- For One Sentece Pitch: This one sentence pitch: [paste your draft] needs to be more impactful and memorable.

Bonus
Let's simulate the investor grilling.

AI Prompt:

> You are a panel of 3 different investors with distinct personalities:
> - The CFO's Nightmare (ROI Obsessive)
> - The Market Validator: Customers, customers, customers. Market fit? Acquisition costs?
> - The Sci-Fi Geek (Visionary)
>
> I'm pitching my [business]. Now for the elevator pitch: [paste what you had written for the elevator pitch before]
>
> CFOs want safety. Validators want proof. Visionaries want legacy.

Each investor should ask me 2 challenging but fair questions about my business based on their personality. Format as:
- Financial Skeptic:
- - Question 1
- - Question 2
- Market Validator:
- - Question 1
- - Question 2
- Visionary:
- - Question 1
- - Question 2

Then provide guidance on how I should prepare to answer these types of questions effectively.

CONCLUSION
IF YOU DO NOT WANT TO BECOME THE NEXT
BLOCKBUSTER, DO NOT CLOSE THIS BOOK YET.

Remember **Blockbuster Video**—*home video giant*.

Laughing stock now. They actually scoffed at mail-order DVDs. **Netflix**? Streaming? *"Never gonna work."*

Now **Blockbuster** is a cautionary tale. A relic. A punchline. Why? They ignored the tidal wave crashing toward them. Missed the memo completely. Now they're a joke. A has-been.

Don't. Be. Blockbuster.

Right now, AI is the exact same wave **Blockbuster** ignored.

That future is loud, and it is changing everything in the present. Imaging industries changed, jobs automated and tonnes of opportunities. This train is leaving the station. Get on, see it zoom off from the sidelines or ride it later when it's overloaded? Your choice.

Future belongs to change embracers. Business. Side hustles. Even YOU—personal growth. All tangled up with AI. The new changes are not a temporary shift but a deep system reset. The potential? Barely scratched.

Recognize how much of an advantage you have gotten. You came here because of your initial curiosity and now you have the necessary keys to open a wonderful future. You have the necessary knowledge and skill. The time to put them to use actively towards making your vision of the future a reality is NOW.

But heads up. Knowledge without action? You have a **Ferrari** parked in your garage. Looks good, goes nowhere.

JOHN VERSUS SARAH.

Let's talk about John. Nice guy. Loves a good spreadsheet. He devoured this book— emphasized like half of it, bought a fancy *"AI Brainstorming"* notebook. Problem is?

The problem is that John is still brainstorming. He's hunting one more tool, one more course, maybe a full moon ritual. He's waiting for the universe to greenlight his launch. He's waiting for a cosmic sign to launch. He's been "almost ready" since dial-up internet. John—buddy—we love the enthusiasm. But you would make **Blockbuster** look decisive. ***Out Blockbustering Blockbuster.***

Enter Sarah—force of nature in human form. She skimmed this book (skipped a bit, who cares?), fired up an AI tool, and launched a digital product before John's spreadsheet hit page two. No way, is it a perfect product. However, it is making money—You bet. Sarah knows done trumps perfect. Iteration is queen. Sometimes there is no other way to go with it than to dive in headfirst. Her secret—imperfect action beats perfect paralysis.

Fast forward six months. John: Still optimizing his "launch checklist." Still procrastinating. His money worries grow. Sarah? Her digital product is live. It brings in cash. She learns constantly. Improves constantly. She is ACTUALLY building financial freedom rather than dreaming about it.

So what's the takeaway here?

Simple: accept the chaos as Sarah and go, launch when you're not yet ready. For the love of heavens—stop over analyzing everything. Those who wait for the perfect moment miss the perfect moment. SPOILER: ***There IS NO perfect moment.*** Don't be John!

> *This one principle—***relentless action***—heart of every self-help book EVER. Seriously. It all boils down to this. Read it 10 times. Repeat daily. Make love to it. Tattoo it to your brain. Until you STOP overthinking. (You're welcome!)*

The future is bright. AI's a moving target. Yesterday's trick is tomorrow's history. That's why being a continuous learner is the most valuable skill to develop. This challenge should not be the end of your AI education. This book was just the starting line.

Want to stay ahead? My <u>newsletter</u>. It's got the real talk. Too spicy for this book. Too potent for print — **yspweb.com/newsletter**

ALSO...

Remember the quiz?

An interactive quiz will help you discover your ideal AI income path if you have not yet taken it. Get matched AND access an exclusive course.

Link's right here: **go.yspweb.com/quiz**

Final thought—2000—**Blockbuster** could've bought **Netflix** for $50 million—they laughed all the way to bankruptcy. Today **Netflix** is worth hundreds of billions.

Meanwhile...

90% of "AI Experts" are still watching YouTube tutorials.
Don't be a statistic.
Take action.

Your Honest Take?
Funds My Coffee
Addiction
(It's Important)

Did you realise 97% of indie authors persist on *reader reviews* in order to survive? I made that last bit up, but the point was clear.

I am already at it writing my next book. Before that, however, you need to weigh in on this. ***Honestly.***

Look: You liked the book? ***Fantastic.*** Tell someone. *Anyone.* Leave an *honest review.* Or just a *star rating.* To do so, simply scroll to the customer reviews section on its product page. ***Your feedback is gold.*** Small authors like yours truly need your support. I offer a small number of *beta copies* of my upcoming release to readers who want to provide feedback before publication. If you want to join as a *beta reader* reach me at tigran@yspweb.com

Boom! With that, you are now an official *beta reader* with *exclusive access.*

Scan this QR code for *1 CLICK STAR RATING:*

Make an Author Smile

Didn't click for you? Happens. My email is tigran@yspweb.com so contact me there for any questions. Maybe I can help. Maybe you have ideas.

Dialogue is good.
Always.

Let's find the resources. That will get you there.

Make an Author Smile

REFERENCES

Generative AI to become a $1.3 trillion market by 2032, Research Finds | Press | Bloomberg LP. (2023, June 1). Bloomberg L.P. https://www.bloomberg.com/company/press/generative-ai-to-become-a-1-3-trillion-market-by-2032-research-finds/

PricewaterhouseCoopers. (n.d.). *PwC's Global Artificial Intelligence Study: Sizing the prize.* PwC. https://www.pwc.com/gx/en/issues/data-and-analytics/publications/artificial-intelligence-study.html

AI in Decision Making Statistics Statistics: ZIPDO Education Reports 2024. (n.d.). https://zipdo.co/ai-in-decision-making-statistics/

Hern, A. (2024, April 9). Elon Musk predicts superhuman AI will be smarter than people next year. *The Guardian.* https://www.theguardian.com/technology/2024/apr/09/elon-musk-predicts-superhuman-ai-will-be-smarter-than-people-next-year

Heikkilä, M. (2023, November 27). Unpacking the hype around OpenAI's rumored new Q* model. *MIT Technology Review.* https://www.technologyreview.com/2023/11/27/1083886/unpacking-the-hype-around-openais-rumored-new-q-model/

Fei, N., Lu, Z., Gao, Y., Yang, G., Huo, Y., Wen, J., Lu, H., Song, R., Gao, X., Xiang, T., Sun, H., and Wen, J. (2022). Towards artificial general intelligence via a multimodal foundation model. *Nature Communications, 13*(1). https://doi.org/10.1038/s41467-022-30761-2

Muthuraj, N., and Singla, N. S. (2023). Artificial intelligence and machine learning. *Medico-Legal Update, 23*(5), 6–11. https://doi.org/10.37506/mlu.v23i5.3458

Moore-Colyer, R. (2024, April 24). Claude 3 Opus has stunned AI researchers with its intellect and "self-awareness" — does this mean it can think for... *livescience.com.* https://www.livescience.com/technology/artificial-intelligence/anthropic-claude-3-opus-stunned-ai-researchers-self-awareness-does-this-mean-it-can-think-for-itself

Gen AI is passé. Enter the age of agentic AI. (2024, July 27). SiliconANGLE. https://siliconangle.com/2024/06/29/gen-ai-passe-enter-age-agentic-ai/

Google Brain founder Andrew Ng says threat of AI causing human extinction is overblown. (2023, November 1). SiliconANGLE. https://siliconangle.com/2023/10/31/google-brain-founder-andrew-ng-says-threat-ai-causing-human-extinction-overblown/

Privacy in an AI era: How do we protect our personal information? (2024, March 18). Stanford HAI. https://hai.stanford.edu/news/privacy-ai-era-how-do-we-protect-our-personal-information

Hern, A. (2024, May 25). Big tech has distracted world from existential risk of AI, says top scientist. *The Guardian.* https://www.theguardian.com/technology/article/2024/may/25/big-tech-existential-risk-ai-scientist-max-tegmark-regulations

Davies, P. (2024, February 26). Open source vs closed source AI: What's the difference and why does it matter? *Euronews.* https://www.euronews.com/next/2024/02/20/open-source-vs-closed-source-ai-whats-the-difference-and-why-does-it-matter

Heaven, W. D. (2023, June 21). Predictive policing algorithms are racist. They need to be dismantled. *MIT Technology Review.* https://www.technologyreview.com/2020/07/17/1005396/predictive-policing-algorithms-racist-dismantled-machine-learning-bias-criminal-justice/

Mattu, J. a. L. K. (2023, December 20). Machine bias. *ProPublica.* https://www.propublica.org/article/machine-bias-risk-assessments-in-criminal-sentencing

Eevis. (2023, March 11). *The language we use matters.* DEV Community. https://dev.to/eevajonnapanula/the-language-we-use-matters-9mn

Thomas, C. (2014, September 14). *Deer Detection with Machine Learning Part 3.* Craig Thomas. https://craigthomas.ca/blog/2014/09/14/deer-detection-with-machine-learning-part-3/

Bohannon, M. (2023, June 8). Lawyer used ChatGPT in Court—And cited fake cases. A judge is considering sanctions. *Forbes.* https://www.forbes.com/sites/mollybohannon/2023/06/08/lawyer-used-chatgpt-in-court-and-cited-fake-cases-a-judge-is-considering-sanctions/

Grant, N. (2024, February 26). Google Chatbot's A.I. images put people of color in Nazi-Era uniforms. *The*

REFERENCES

New York Times. https://www.nytimes.com/2024/02/22/technology/google-gemini-german-uniforms.html

Lenrow, D. (2024, May 30). The Limits of Working Memory: Human Brains vs. AI Models. *Illumio Cybersecurity Blog | Illumio*. https://www.illumio.com/blog/the-limits-of-working-memory-human-brains-vs-ai-models

Crabtree, M. (2024, January 12). *What is Prompt Engineering? A Detailed Guide For 2024*. https://www.datacamp.com/blog/what-is-prompt-engineering-the-future-of-ai-communication

Ho, I. (2024, March 18). Automated Prompt Engineering - towards data science. *Medium*. https://towardsdatascience.com/automated-prompt-engineering-78678c6371b9

(6) Alex Albert on X: "Lots of LLMs are good at code, but Claude 3 Opus is the first model I've used that's very good at prompt engineering as well. Here's the workflow I use for prompt engineering in tandem with Opus:" / X. (n.d.). X (Formerly Twitter). https://twitter.com/alexalbert__/status/1767258557039378511

Rojo-Echeburúa, A. (2024, July 9). *Prompt chaining tutorial: What is prompt chaining and how to use it?* https://www.datacamp.com/tutorial/prompt-chaining-llm

Fire, A. (n.d.). *Discover why AI search engines are better than Google*. AI Fire. https://www.aifire.co/p/discover-why-ai-search-engines-are-better-than-google

Pr, A., and Pr, A. (2024, July 1). *VakilAI unveils groundbreaking AI legal Companion for lawyers and law firms*. ThePrint. https://theprint.in/ani-press-releases/vakilai-unveils-groundbreaking-ai-legal-companion-for-lawyers-and-law-firms/2155165/

Bhatia, S. (2024, June 3). Anticipating the Future: How AI will impact businesses in 2024. *Forbes*. https://www.forbes.com/sites/forbestechcouncil/2024/02/21/anticipating-the-future-how-ai-will-impact-businesses-in-2024/

How AI is Revolutionizing Market Research? (n.d.). UXpilot.ai. https://uxpilot.ai/blogs/ai-revolutionizing-market-research

Boufous, M. (2024, April 11). *10 Ways to use AI in Competitive Analysis*. Marketing. https://www.panoramata.co/benchmark-marketing/ai-competitive-analysis

Chesson, D. (2024, April 20). *The most searched Amazon Keywords and trends in 2024*. Kindlepreneur. https://kindlepreneur.com/most-searched-amazon-keywords-trends-2024/

Windisch, C. P. a. M. (2023, December 4). *What's next for copyright in the age of artificial intelligence?* ProMarket. https://www.promarket.org/2023/12/12/whats-next-for-copyright-in-the-age-of-artificial-intelligence/

Everything a writer needs to know about AI and copyrights. (2024, July 22). The Urban Writers. https://theurbanwriters.com/blogs/publishing/copyrighting-ai-content-what-you-need-to-know-as-a-writer

Lando and Anastasi, LLP. (2024, February 12). *IP Considerations for AI-Generated Content: Copyrights and Beyond | Lando and Anastasi, LLP*. https://www.lalaw.com/knowledge-center/article/ip-considerations-for-ai-generated-content-copyrights-and-beyond/

Adams, R. (2017, July 6). The 7 elements of an irresistibly compelling offer. *Entrepreneur*. https://www.entrepreneur.com/growing-a-business/the-7-elements-of-an-irresistibly-compelling-offer/296150

Panel, E. (2023, March 30). 14 tips for crafting Attention-Grabbing headlines. *Forbes*. https://www.forbes.com/sites/forbescommunicationscouncil/2023/03/30/14-tips-for-crafting-attention-grabbing-headlines/

Ellis, M. (2023, October 24). *2024 Amazon Book Rankings Explained: How to Estimate and Improve sales*. Niche Pursuits. https://www.nichepursuits.com/amazon-book-rankings-explained/

Made in the USA
Monee, IL
18 June 2025

19588931R00085